MW00640648

THE BOOK DIRECT BLUEPRINT

MARK SIMPSON

Instagram.com/boostlyuk

Facebook.com/boostlyuk

Linkedin.com/in/mrmarksimpson/

Twitter.com/boostlyuk

CONTENTS

Instagram.com/boostlyuk

Facebook.com/boostlyuk

Linkedin.com/in/mrmarksimpson/

Twitter.com/boostlyuk

SPEAK LIKE A PRO

OTA	Online Travel Agency (the likes of Airbnb, Booking.com, etc)
STR	Short Term Rental (the UK term for 'vacation rentals')
PMS	Property Management Software
GID	Get It Done
SEO	Search Engine Optimisation
CTA	Call To Action
DM	Direct Message / Private Message
FPG	Future Potential Guest

Let me know that you're
reading this book.

Send me a message on

Instagram.com/boostlyuk

INTRODUCTION

NEVER BUILD YOUR HOUSE ON SOMEONE ELSE'S LAND

The irony of life is that you learn most of its lessons after making the mistakes.

Since the dawn of civilisation, human beings have been learning from their own mistakes. Sometimes paying the price with money, sometimes paying the price with discomfort.

A toddler learns how to walk after bruising their knee half a dozen times. A business leader learns the importance of accountancy after drowning in a pile of receipts. And for the most part, a short-term rental host learns the value of direct bookings after letting an OTA drain their bank balance.

And while these mistakes make you endure that temporary pain-in-the-arse kind of feeling, they're worth their weight in gold. So long as you recognise their value soon enough and implement whatever they teach you.

I think a lot of the negative connotations we associate with the word "mistake" are because of societal conditioning and, perhaps, a lack of self-belief. But when you train your mind to realise that every setback is an opportunity to get better (and getting better isn't something you need to do alone), then you begin to embrace every "error" as an experience.

Every bruise as a blessing.

And every questionable decision as something you can keep aside for a better time and purpose.

This book is the result of a similar kind of bad decision.

I will tell you why.

You see, when I was writing my debut book, *The Book Direct Playbook*, I put together a chapter which covered everything a short-term rental host needs to set up "behind-the-scenes" to eliminate their reliance on OTAs. Those few thousand words were edited, proofread and ready to go.

Then, at the last moment, I pulled that chapter from the *Playbook*.

It was a combination of imposter syndrome and the words in that chapter not doing the topic justice. I'm a big believer in people staying in their own lane and talking about areas in which they have the most knowledge and expertise, as a way of offering honest value to their audience.

So, believing that chapter was a "bad decision" for the *Playbook* at that time, I set it aside and allowed my debut book to be a jam-packed collection of marketing tips and tactics. I knew that I'd find a reason to revisit that other singled-out chapter some other time.

And that was that. Soon after, *The Book Direct Playbook* was published, and it was a roaring success.

★★★

Not long after my debut author experience, I was offered the opportunity to be part of a fantastic multi-author book *Hospitable Hosts*, by Jodie Stirling. The book cleverly collated over forty stories from various short-term rental hosts and took the industry by storm.

I learned so much from my own contribution as a co-author and it was this experience that inspired a new idea for my stagnant chapter. Finally, I had realised how I could bring it to life and do it justice.

Much like Jodie Stirling, I have been very fortunate since setting up Boostly, as the journey has allowed me to work with some of the strongest and most talented minds. Whether it be through Boostly's podcast interviews, or the direct booking websites Boostly creates for short-term rental hosts, I have seen firsthand how our industry is packed-to-the-seams with expertise.

Expertise that would simply go to waste if not captured correctly.

So, with that in mind, one sunny July morning (with a pot of fresh coffee at hand), I sketched out the areas of a short-term rental business that every host needs to have in place to ensure they have the foundations of a successful direct bookings business.

I revisited the chapter I had set aside and thought about the numerous experts in our industry.

The more I looked at it, the more the reality of it dawned on me.

How had I not seen it all along?

A blueprint.

A blueprint is what I was looking at. And that realisation alone filled my insides with excitement!

All the research notes that I'd mapped out were essentially the foundations of a floor plan – very similar to what you'd find if you were building your short-term rental home from the ground up. Just imagine an architect showing you all the details that need to be in place to build your new venture.

The brickwork, the walls, the roof.

There's no point adding a fancy living room to your property, with floor-to-ceiling windows, if you don't add doors in the right areas to access it.

And that is why blueprints exist.

So, while I don't plan on donning a builder's hat just yet, I'd like to present you with your own "blueprint", specifically designed for a successful short-term rental business, which doesn't rely on OTAs. As per my inspiration, I have handpicked some of our industry's most knowledgeable and experienced leaders to help put this together for you – so that you have the biggest chance of success in nailing *every* area of direct bookings.

For those of you who have read my debut book, *The Book Direct Playbook*, you'll know that I'm a big fan of comic book movies. Well, these STR heroes, whom I'm going to put before you over the next few chapters, are my Avengers. The best of the best, who will guide you through your short-term rental journey – whether you're looking to start up, scale, or sell your business in the future. And they will do so by keeping direct bookings at the helm of everything.

A few mistakes, bad choices, and cups of coffee later, things haven't turned out bad at all, have they?

It just goes to show how much we can grow when we open our minds to learning.

ABOUT THIS BOOK

Who Not How by Dan Sullivan is a book that I've gifted to hundreds of short-term rental hosts and business owners.

The title of the book rings in my head as a quote more than once a day.

If you've not had a chance to read this masterpiece, it explores the question you normally ask yourself when facing a problem in your life or business:

"How am I going to achieve (or solve) this?"

In the book, Sullivan encourages readers to rephrase that question to:

"Who can I bring in to help me achieve this right now?"

What I've decided to do with *The Book Direct Blueprint* is the epitome of the above. And, hopefully, you'll find its multi-authored and "multi-talent" style of great value to you. Each chapter – whether it be about **Pricing** to **Property Management Software** to **Creating the Best Guest Experience** – has been curated by the authors themselves. And, if you're a book geek, you will definitely enjoy the change in tone-of-voice and style in each section (it keeps things exciting, for sure).

★★★

Another thing that you might have picked up on if you've read *The Book Direct Playbook* is that I rarely read books from beginning to end. For me, information is much easier to digest when it's in bite-sized chunks and laid out in a way that enables me to dive in and out, whenever I want.

I'm sure a number of time-poor short-term rental hosts like you are on a similar wavelength.

So, don't worry if you don't have two hours set aside to study a chunky book because that is not what this book is. I have specifically designed *The Book Direct Blueprint* to be easily scannable, user-friendly (even if you're on the move) and not something that needs to be read in order. In fact, if you feel that there's an area of business that you're struggling with most, feel free to skip to the chapter that covers that first. You are completely in control of how you learn here.

You might also like to look up one of my favourite Instagram follows and superstar Boostly client @mykaartis and take a leaf out of his book. He documents the books he's reading (on a daily basis) and simply reads ten pages at a time.

Of course, you're more than welcome to read *The Book Direct Blueprint* from beginning to end if that's what you prefer. But please note that it caters to a wide scope of readers and doesn't intend to test your patience, in any way.

ALLOW ME TO REINTRODUCE MYSELF

In case you haven't read *The Book Direct Playbook*, allow me to tell you a bit about myself and the mission that I've taken on.

My name is Mark Simpson and I give hosts all over the world the tools, tactics, training and, most importantly, the confidence to boost their direct bookings.

My mission is a simple one. To help one million hosts and STR business owners cut down on their overreliance on Airbnb and other online travel agencies.

This self-proclaimed obsession began over ten years ago, when my wife and I moved back to my family business (The Grainary) in Scarborough, UK. It was there that I realised the astonishing lack of support for hospitality businesses on a local (and accessible) level.

This inspired the inception of Boostly. I like to think of myself as a doer; if there's a problem that I know I can solve, then you won't catch me wasting time complaining about it. And so, Boostly grew from strength to strength in full force, taking vast numbers of STR hosts under its rocket ship wing and helping them generate more direct bookings.

It's been a ride, all right.

To date, the Boostly Website Company remains one of the largest agencies of its kind in the world, and our Training Academy is one of the *only* officially accredited academies for the short-term rental industry. This is all with enormous thanks to my team, and all the talented people who work so hard behind the scenes. One of whom I'm so excited to showcase to you in this book!

Throughout my career, I've had the honour of professionally speaking at some of the biggest hospitality events across the globe. I'm also the host of an award-winning podcast (Boostly Podcast), which is frequently ranked in the top podcast charts.

While it might sound like I'm a non-stop workaholic at this point, I should tell you my family is at the pinnacle of everything that I do. When I wrote *The Book Direct Playbook*, I had three brilliant boys, Alfie, Charlie and Frankie.

And now, at the time of writing this book, we have welcomed a beautiful baby girl called Rosie to our tribe.

Speaking of family, I wanted to reserve a special mention for my wife,

Laura Nicholson Simpson, without whom my debut book *The Book Direct Playbook* would have never seen the light of day. Not only because she was an incredible support and mother to our children (while I put the extra hours in for writing), but because just before I submitted the final draft of that manuscript – in line with my publisher's strict deadline – Laura swooped in to save the day. At the time, something didn't feel right about the book. And so, my wife (who is an unbelievable jack-of-all-trades) put in forty-eight hours straight to help me polish up the book, perfect it and proofread it. The debut book moment would have ceased to exist without Laura; so, this little section is dedicated entirely to her.

Thank you, Laura.

SPADES IN THE GROUND

All right, it's finally time to get started and get your spades in the ground.

I will now take a back seat and pass the baton to my trusted Avengers, who will talk you through their areas of expertise. Each of them is a master in their own right, so rest assured, you'll be polishing up your knowledge in various areas of the short-term rentals industry (and what it takes to generate more direct bookings).

I will occasionally "pop in" to see how you're getting on with the book and share some additional insights, where relevant.

And, if you're listening on Audible, get ready for a special guest who I've lined up especially to help narrate the words from our authors.

You're truly in for an epic treat. So, if you want to grab a copy of *The Book Direct Blueprint* on Audible, then simply open the app and search for "Book Direct Blueprint". This will also help you tap into a low-key genius productivity hack that I've learned over the years. That is: to listen to books on Audible while reading them at the same time. (Trust me, you will retain loads more information this way.)

Also, to help you become an even stronger short-term rentals superstar, this *Blueprint* is accompanied by an online course that the team and I have specially created for you. In it, you'll find tutorial videos, interviews with our authors and genius tools that you can use in your business straight away. Best of all, it's free.

All you need to do is head to **bookdirectblueprint.com**

THE
BOOK DIRECT
BLUEPRINT

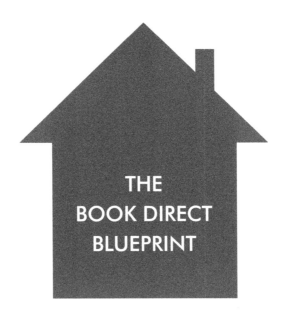

| TRUST, FIRST

I-PRAC

In a small town, just outside of London, lived a well-to-do family of five. The parents (the father the more risk averse of the two), their teenage children and a pet Labrador named Jimmy.

It was coming close to the summer holiday season. And as per annual tradition, the family were gathered around the kitchen dining table, planning their next trip.

Venice was the city of choice this year. The family was much looking forward to exploring this wonderland of canals, visiting the Bridge of Sighs and the city's famous Venetian Ghetto, as well as nibbling on some cicchetti, of course.

There was just the important matter of accommodation to settle.

The father opened a new tab on his web browser and instinctively typed "airbnb.com" into the address bar. This was the usual protocol, after all, as the family had been booking holiday rentals for years.

"Here we are," he proudly piped up. "Easy. List of options just within our budget. Which do you like the look of?"

The mother, who was busy scrolling on her own tablet, peered over from her glasses and smiled. "I've found a gorgeous short-term rental, near the best tourist spots. It says the rates are substantially lower if we book direct. Come, take a look."

Her husband glanced over the handheld tablet and dismissed it within seconds. "I've never heard of this company. Why not just book with a well-known name, like we always do? Did you hear that the Ahmeds next door got absolutely cleaned out by a phoney STR company? They paid thousands for accommodation that didn't even exist! Apparently, the company had a pretty convincing-looking website. I'd rather spend the extra money with Airbnb."

By now, Jimmy was pacing up and down the dining room area, clearly keen to be taken for his walk. Knowing that time was of the essence, the mother clicked on the "Trust Page" of the short-term rental's website, and gestured the tablet towards her husband. "Look. It says they're I-PRAC approved. And they've explained what that means… right here."

Both the parents huddled over the tablet and read the company's Trust Page with interest.

"So, they guarantee full payment protection?" the father asked (now feeling reassured).

"That's right," his wife replied. "But I-PRAC Accreditation also guarantees that this property is legitimate and meets very high professional standards. Look, here's a photo of the owners, too – you have to admit, it would be nice to book accommodation with a company that actually has a face, right? Remember Airbnb's thread of automated emails when we had an issue with that apartment in Santorini last year?"

With a unanimous sigh of relief, both parents confirmed their two-week booking, directly on the short-term rental's website.

"Saved a good few quid there, too!" the father happily announced.

"It'll be nice to focus all our energies on looking forward to our Italian getaway now," his wife replied. "I can't remember the last time I felt so at ease before going away."

Her husband pulled her in for a soft kiss on the forehead. "That's the value of trust, sweety. Come, let's go and tell the kids."

Some Inarguable Truths

While the above account is fictional and we do not personally know of a Labrador named Jimmy, the story represents the many frequent conversations that occur within families behind closed doors.

In the story, the father did not even think twice before starting his holiday accommodation search on an OTA's website. This was largely to do with habit, brand familiarity, and what he had deciphered as feelings of "trust" towards Airbnb.

His wife, on the other hand, offered an alternative option, which was better for several reasons and, most importantly, eliminated any kind of uncertainty. Ultimately, the parents decided to book directly with the short-term rental property because the company offered a clear guarantee via I-PRAC Approval and, therefore, ultimate peace of mind and protection for the entire family.

Our story really does beg the question: why do we muddle up our priorities in business so much?

Take the matter of generating more direct bookings as an example. Thanks to overhyped trends, unusual TikTok challenges, and the rise of the self-proclaimed branding experts, our industry is at risk of falling out of touch with the things that matter most.

Meaningful business relationships.

Brand loyalty and reputation.

Trust.

You could spend thousands on a flash direct bookings website that will showcase your properties from the most stunning angles. But if you skip the part that cements trust with your target guests, then filling up your calendar will be about as difficult as teaching a fish to ride a bicycle.

This is a simple life lesson. Whether you outwardly realise it or not, trust is at the pinnacle of every decision you make.

The reason you choose to buy your morning coffee from one café as opposed to another is because you trust their delivery will be better in some way.

The reason you choose for your children to enrol in a particular school is because you trust that school will offer them a better quality education.

The reason you choose to settle down with a lifetime spouse is because you trust that person will make you happy.

Even something as futile as adding an extra pinch of salt to your casserole before serving it is because you trust (in this case, your own gut instinct) that the dish will taste better as a result of the modification. So, when it comes to the subject of booking a short-term rental property (one that is likely to ask guests to part with a substantial amount of cash), then of course the emotion of trust will steer and determine the entire booking process.

Giving away money and the best part of a holiday or business experience is no small ordeal for any person. And if paying guests do not trust a particular short-term rental provider to deliver, then you can bet that they will browse through the thousands of other options on the market, even if it means having to pay a higher booking fee.

So, before focusing on any other area of branding, marketing or PR for your short-term rental business, make it your priority to now understand the unavoidable importance of trust psychology and trust marketing. Without doing this, your chances of competing – and winning – against the OTAs are slim.

The Neuroscience of Trust

The psychology of trust is deep-rooted enough to flesh out an entire book, let alone a single chapter.

We have come a long way in the short-term rental industry, with more people drawing upon the significance of trust, yet even today, we have barely scratched the surface.

At I-PRAC, we deploy something called "trust marketing". This is closely related to emotional marketing, a term that the majority of hospitality business leaders have come across before. For us, trust marketing targets our audience's emotions first and foremost because it is a well-known fact that consumers **buy on emotion and justify with logic.**

To believe otherwise, and to simply throw clinical strategies at your sales funnels, is practically direct bookings suicide. Neuroscience itself explains that the decision to buy (anything) is made subconsciously, and these subconscious decisions are based on a deeply empirical mental processing system.

When a guest views your property, they quickly come to an intuitive decision whether or not to book with you – and this is communicated to the conscious mind via an emotion. The emotion, in this case, is largely trust.

Then, the guest's conscious mind searches for rational reasons to book with you (such as details of price, location and amenities) and that is how they complete the circle. Ultimately, the guest justifies their emotional signals with logical reasons – the pragmatism of their decision-making is actually "secondary", which is why so many wise business mentors will advise you to never compete with things like price if you want to build a scalable direct bookings business.

"95% of purchasing decisions take place unconsciously. And yet, when we seek to persuade buyers, we sell almost exclusively to Mr or Ms Rationale and wonder why transactions get stuck in paralysis."

– (paraphrased from Harvard Business Review)

Narrowing down to the emotion of trust, some of the biggest brands in the world have taken this magic ingredient and sprinkled it all over their companies to boldly dominate market shares.

The big players such as Amazon, Apple and Airbnb realise that marketing is a game of human psychology; by using the right proof, processes, stories and "trust signals", they can not only determine a few quick sales, but *repeat sales* that could potentially last a customer's entire lifetime.

When a person feels the emotion of trust, their brain releases a chemical called oxytocin, also commonly known as "the love drug". Oxytocin is the same chemical that is released when mothers bond with their babies, and within two people when they are falling in love. Scientific studies have proved that when we have a greater amount of oxytocin in our brain, our levels of empathy, compassion and love increase too, putting us in an ideal state of mind to form long-lasting relationships and behave in a more receptive way.

The science speaks for itself. Earning the trust of your guests will be far more profitable for you in the long-term than high-res photography and lists of social media hashtags. While the latter is also important, remember that shiny aesthetics and empty words bring guests to your front door. But well-earned feelings of trust actually get them to knock on it and spend money with you.

Eliminating Uncertainty

"Uncertainty is the killer of conversion" – make this one of your biggest business mantras when scaling your short-term rental business.

These powerful words, from I-PRAC's CEO Chris Maughan himself, are rooted in years' worth of psychological and behavioural study.

Essentially, this quote helps us understand why eliminating uncertainty from a guest's mind is the difference between more direct bookings and empty calendars (unless, of course, those calendars are sponsored by OTAs).

Whether we like it or not, the human brain biologically encourages bad news, bad thoughts and bad events to linger. Parts of our brain, like the amygdala, are hardwired to seek out negativity, and once our brain comes across a potential risk, it commits it to its long-term memory. The colloquial term for this is "survive brain"; it's the survive brain's job to protect us from harm. However, the problem is that the survive brain also suffers from something called "negativity bias", which means that it often overestimates threats and tries to convince us to stay away from the unknown.

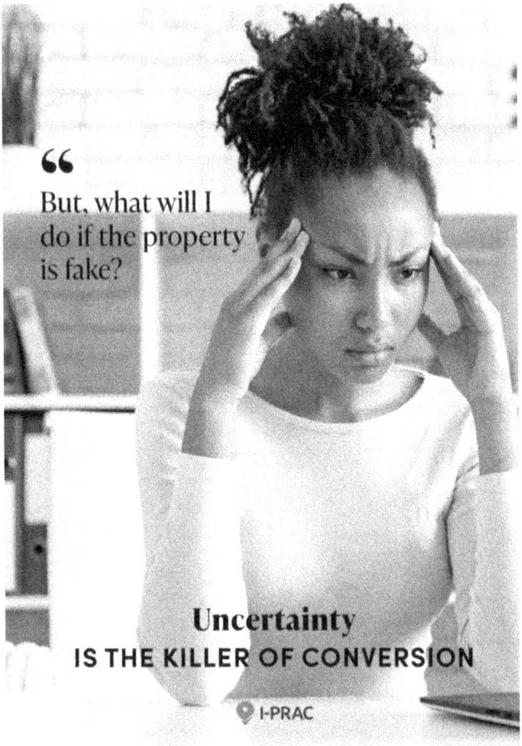

For the majority of guests, OTAs such as Airbnb will be the norm. Your short-term rental property, on the other hand, will be *the unknown* – regardless of the beautiful artwork on your website. This naturally means you have to work harder to eliminate any feelings of uncertainty from your guests' minds, before even thinking about selling a product to them.

A brilliant example of this is Uber, a global app that has disrupted (and dominated) the taxi industry, by eliminating every element of uncertainty for its customers. The irony here is that the company hasn't really reinvented the wheel in any way. The core of Uber's service is simply picking up passengers from a specified location and dropping them off at their desired destination – like any other taxi firm. However, the reason people now opt for Uber over any other telephone taxi company in a heartbeat is because Uber has drastically eliminated risk factors and "threats" in several ways:

- A real-time map and timer, showing customers exactly how long their taxi is going to be, rather than them aimlessly waiting, wondering if their ride will even turn up at all.
- A clear photograph and description of the driver, putting customers at ease.
- Secure and seamless payment methods.
- A guarantee that Uber is fully protected and insured.

The app even allows customers who aren't riding in the Uber, but would like to ensure that their loved ones are safe, to track family members and friends. As such, even with the company's frequent price surges, Uber is highly likely to keep its global customer base and continue to dominate the market.

If you find that guests are failing to follow through with the entire booking process on your direct bookings website, then ask yourself what potential risks are they foreseeing, which you're failing to address. As soon as you put these concerns to rest, you'll strengthen the relationship of trust between you and your audience, and will likely see a sharp increase in your conversion rates.

That's the commercial power of eliminating uncertainty.

Competing with the Trusted OTAs

Since the exponential growth of the short-term rental industry, the likes of Airbnb and Booking.com have been pulling the puppet strings of property hosts and managers worldwide. While these hospitality giants are the "common enemy" for most operators, they have contributed massively to our industry and no doubt helped turn many people's lives around. It is easy to hate them. But if you want to build a direct bookings business, you're better off learning from them instead.

I-PRAC's CEO, Chris Maughan, actually founded his own short-term rental company in Cannes over twenty years ago. The company "AES Events" provides luxury business accommodation across the South of France and has been built entirely in the absence of OTAs.

As far as the industry is concerned, there is no better person to seek guidance from about direct bookings than Chris Maughan, as he is one of the very few operators who has *never* relied on the likes of Airbnb or Booking.com. Not even once. Maughan has built a multi-million-pound short-term rental business from scratch and acquired numerous high-paying clients including MTV, Google, Disney, Spotify, Twitter, Paramount, Netflix and more. These clients have forged long-term relationships with Maughan and his team, and ask for AES Events by name every time they are staying in the South of France for business.

If you were to ask our CEO the "secret" to building a multi-million-pound short-term rental business, then he will tell you in a heartbeat that he acquired his success through sheer hard work, consistency and trust marketing.

PRODUCT MARKETING	TRUST MARKETING
Drives enquiries (interest and leads towards your direct booking website, through pushing products and services)	**Converts into sales (bookings)** (this does not include talking about the product; but rather why a brand can be trusted)*

***Maughan recommends that companies implement both product and trust marketing, simultaneously, across all campaigns.**

During an age when the luxury of social media did not even exist, Maughan spent the early years of his business forging long-term relationships with clients, suppliers and partners. These personal relationships are things which he still nurtures today and which he would not be able to do if an OTA was standing between him and his guests as a money-hungry "middleman".

So, the question in this instance is two-fold: why do guests continue to trust OTAs if they are so impersonal, and what can you do as a short-term rental operator to win the trust of your guests, like our CEO?

Remarkably, even after the negative press about Brian Chesky following Airbnb's post-pandemic announcements, and all the horror stories we read about disastrous Airbnb stays, the OTA is trusted by millions of guests. So dominant has this brand become that when guests book a stay at your property via Airbnb, they will tell their friends that they are "staying at an Airbnb" and most likely not even remember the name of your business.

If the same guests encounter a problem with your property, it will be Airbnb they will contact for assistance and Airbnb who will swoop in to save the day (most likely at your expense). Even on the opposite end of the spectrum, if the guests absolutely adore their stay at your property, it is Airbnb they will positively tag in their social media posts before they even think to mention you.

All this, and you have the privilege of paying the OTA's rising commission fees, too. It does make you wonder, if you run your short-term rental business largely on OTAs, then do you even have a short-term rental business at all?

In simple terms: No.

But what are you expected to do when travellers from every corner of the world type "Airbnb" into their address bar every time they want to book a short-term rental stay?

The first thing you need to understand about OTAs like Airbnb is that they have caught guests hook, line and sinker. Their large marketing budgets mean they have a shortcut to earning the perceived trust of people, as they can make their brand visible everywhere with the help of sponsored ads, flash TV advertisements, costly PR and click-bait campaigns such as the "SuperHost" facade.

Naturally, the more we see something as human beings, the more familiar we become with it. And familiarity is a huge part of generating trust, which is why guests continue to book stays with OTAs. It is simply a case of them being exposed to it more, and hearing other people talk about it (which, again, reinforces that feeling of trust).

Why else could it be that brands like Coca-Cola and McDonald's are embedded into most people's childhoods, and something consumers continue returning to, even in an increasingly health-obsessed world?

Frequent brand exposure and repetitive messaging counts for a lot.

Now, some of the most common advice you'll receive about generating more direct bookings is to inform people your rates are lower if they book directly with you. While this is useful advice – and does work on some level – you must remember that blasting a six-line email to your guest database about "cheaper direct booking rates" is not going to solve all your problems.

If your guests are continuously booking their stay with you via an OTA (even after having stayed with you before) then the issue is far more deep-rooted.

The likelihood is that your guests do not trust that the experience of booking directly with you is worth them stepping out of their comfort zones, which is clicking just a few buttons on an OTA's website. If, in this instance, you are blindly trying to lure them in with templated social media posts and text messages that promote the new linen in your guest bedrooms, then you are inadvertently insulting their priorities.

To reiterate one of our earlier points, guests make a subconscious emotional decision to book with you at the earliest stage of the transactional journey. If you want them to switch to your website from a well-known OTA's, you need to tap into their emotional psyche. And, like Coca-Cola, you need to do it often.

Leveraging Trust and Trust Signals

With no barrier-to-entry for the short-term rental industry, it is easy for property hosts to list their accommodation on a poorly constructed website and expect the bookings to come rolling in. Even if that host has decided to cut the cord from OTAs, they will struggle to build a direct bookings business with that strategy alone.

Human beings, by nature, have a defence mechanism. This is wired into our DNA. No matter how much we have evolved from Homo erectus, we are designed to seek out risks and keep our distance from them. So, when you are marketing your short-term rental properties, you need to be aware of the potential risks your guests are trying to avoid (consciously or subconsciously).

Then, you need to ensure that you address these "risk concerns" across your marketing and in your communication with guests. What guests do not directly tell you is that they inadvertently value peace of mind more than anything else. Ultimately, people just want to feel safe. This is one hundred percent the case when you're checking into a stranger's home, which is what the business of short-term rentals essentially is.

Doing the above translates as using trust tools and trust signals across various areas of your short-term rental business.

Rather than blindly creating content for your direct bookings website or uploading a dozen beautiful photos on your Instagram page, start with a solid trust marketing strategy that gives your guests the assurance they need – and the assurance they are so desperately trying to seek on an OTA's website.

According to official research that I-PRAC carried out in 2021 (by asking one hundred randomly selected guests an unbiased question), these are the top concerns of travellers when booking a short-term rental stay:

1. Safety, security and payment protection.
2. Property legitimacy and professional standards.
3. Cleanliness and hygiene.

These findings go against popular belief, as a shocking 85% of property owners still believe cleanliness and hygiene to be the main concerns of short-term rental guests. However, this research proves otherwise.

The findings from this in-house research are gold dust. When you can decipher exactly what risks your target guests are trying to avoid, you can use it to build your short-term rental business around, and give yourself the competitive edge over OTAs.

Remember, this kind of targeted personalisation is something OTAs cannot do, as they are nothing more than booking platforms where STR operators are akin to digits and letters.

Let us take the guests' most pressing concern of safety, security and payment protection. This concern comes as no surprise when travellers have reportedly lost a collective of *millions* in holiday rental fraud, as well as on fake properties posing to be "legitimate" on phoney websites – and even on platforms such as Airbnb.

There is currently no other determining factor other than **I-PRAC Accreditation** that gives guests the assurance they need to one hundred percent trust that the short-term rental provider they're booking with is legitimate, professional and that their payment is fully protected.

OTAs, no matter how well-known or how well-funded, offer no such guarantee.

So, that oxytocin hit that guests are looking for on Airbnb's, Vrbo's and Booking.com's websites can be easily found on yours if your property is I-PRAC Approved and you smartly leverage I-PRAC accreditation as the ultimate trust tool.

Using Your Trust Marketing Tool

As the world's only membership and verification platform for the short-term rental industry, I-PRAC (and more specifically "I-PRAC Approval") translates as a "badge of honour" for short-term rental hosts, following a robust and meticulous verification process.

However, this is far from a pitch to become I-PRAC Approved and simply sit back and watch your short-term rental business grow. The success of your STR empire and the rise of your direct bookings is intrinsically linked to trust. Even going through the process of becoming an I-PRAC member is worth limited value if you do not learn how to leverage the accreditation and use it as the ultimate trust marketing tool.

Think again about a human being's proven tendency to make decisions based on subconscious emotions. And how the emotion of trust (and that all-important oxytocin chemical) is at the helm of every transaction – no matter how big or small.

If you are to place the words "I-PRAC Approved" on the above-the-fold section of your direct bookings website – and explain exactly what that means – then you are immediately positioning yourself as the stronger contender of the short-term rental pack; one your guests will naturally feel more confident to book with.

But this is just the tip of the iceberg. Strategic trust signals across your branding and marketing messages will determine the loyalty between you and your target audience, and help you unshackle yourselves from commission-hungry OTAs.

> Did you know that the bounce rate on most direct bookings websites is highest on the actual booking page (where guests are asked to part with their money)? This is likely because guests do not trust a certain element of the payment process. If you are to mention a **payment protection guarantee** at this stage of the booking process – courtesy of I-PRAC – you will see an immediate rise in complete transactions.

> **According to research from Edelman, 81% of consumers reported in 2021 that they need to trust a brand before spending money with them.** Rather than wasting website space by writing a five-thousand-word story about your personal hobbies and past achievements, create a dedicated **Trust Page** for your website, which explains to guests why they can trust you – as a result of your I-PRAC Accreditation.

> **The journey does not stop after a guest has completed their booking. Ensure that you follow through with your service and delivery; cement that trust for the long-haul.** Little but meaningful gestures, such as handwritten welcome letters and hampers at your property to create some memorable hits of dopamine for your guests, will go a long way. Include your I-PRAC Approved logo on these products to reinforce that you are a trusted brand. A large part of trust building is to actually do what you have said you are going to do. So, if you have promised incredible hospitality on your website and across your marketing, ensure the experience you offer lives up to it.

The Evolution of Guest Behaviour and Expectations

Imagine you are on the way to a watch shop, and a person stops you on the street to sell you a Rolex. Chances are, you will not purchase a Rolex from them because the defence mechanism that's been wired into you will immediately send alert signals to your brain, telling you that there is no way you can trust this Rolex to be genuine. This is regardless of the charm and descriptive sales talk of the Rolex salesperson.

Even today, many hospitality business leaders do the equivalent of these street sellers. They push their products and services to customers via social media and flouncy emails (i.e. through product marketing alone), and make little attempt to create meaningful connections.

While this strategy of "pushing products" might have converted into sales decades ago, you must understand that the market is changing, and consumer behaviour and expectations have evolved.

Recent surveys from a company called **Hubspot** found that only three percent of today's consumers find salespeople and marketeers trustworthy. Strategies built around fear marketing, exposing people's pain points (brutally) and simply listing the unique selling points of a product or service are now increasingly falling on deaf ears.

Millennials and Gen Z guests have become even more challenging to reach, if you do not take the time to understand their values and priorities. In fact, only around one percent of millennials claim that compelling ads influence them – the rest are naturally sceptical of salesy advertisements.

We have now entered a travel landscape whereby guests' expectations are different (and, in many ways, far more sophisticated). A failure to evolve with these times and educate yourself around the benefits of trust signals and tools such as I-PRAC Accreditation can cost you thousands in direct bookings.

For these very reasons, it is vital that you don't make "turning an OTA booking into a direct booking" your goal.

This is a common misconception among many short-term rental hosts, yet one that they are widely taught to pursue – for ill-informed and inaccurate reasons. The presumption that just because a guest has booked your property with an OTA in the past means that they will definitely book directly with you in the future is naive and dismisses the psychological and behavioural aspects of a guest's booking journey.

Returning back to the subject of consumer behaviour – and, in this case, traveller behaviour – also bear in mind that it's highly unlikely for a guest to book the same accommodation (especially for holiday purposes) twice. Of course, this can happen where corporate travel is concerned, but if you are in the business of generating more holiday bookings, then do not make "repeat guests" your goal.

Even if a guest has had an exceptional time at your holiday property, they will want to experience something different on their next trip. In fact, ask yourself this very question: have you ever booked two identical holidays, whereby you've kept all the details, such as destination, accommodation and meal plans exactly the same? How often does this actually happen?

Instead, as a short-term rental operator, your focus should be on collecting recommendations and good old-fashioned word of mouth marketing. When a guest has had a positive experience at your property, they will probably not book with you again any time soon. But they *probably will* post about you on social media and recommend you to family and friends.

In the short-term rental industry, we use the term "Levels of Guest Satisfaction" to explain this concept in full. There are three levels of guest satisfaction, and you should be working towards the third.

1. Did not enjoy the experience, will definitely not return nor recommend.

2. Did enjoy the experience, would consider returning (if the opportunity arises), will not recommend.
3. Did enjoy the experience, would definitely consider returning (if ever planning an identical holiday/stay), absolutely will recommend.

As we have already covered in immense detail in this chapter, an enormous part of guest satisfaction and a positive guest experience is peace of mind, zero uncertainty, and feelings of reassurance. If you achieve this via I-PRAC Approval (and the numerous trust marketing strategies we have outlined), as well as excellent hospitality, then the recommendations are likely to come in thick and fast.

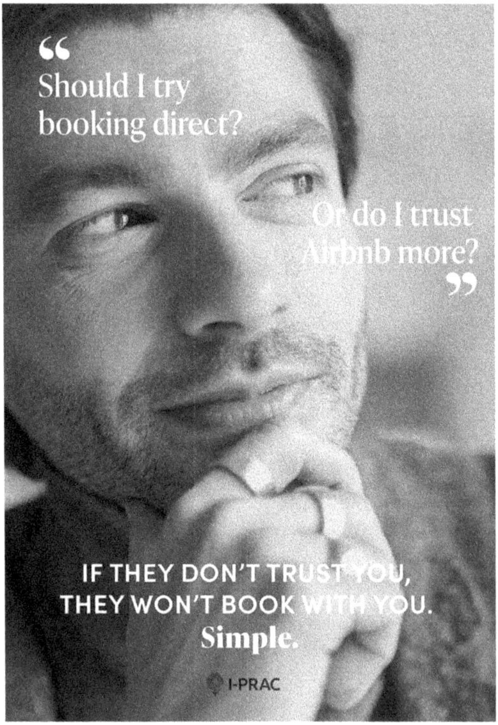

The Future of Direct Bookings is Trust

Since that infamous day in 2014, when our CEO Chris Maughan came face-to-face with a stranded family in the South of France, who had just been conned out of thousands of pounds to holiday rental fraud, solidifying trust across the industry became his primary goal.

But, as you'll have found over the last few thousand words, the concept of trust (and the innate desire for it) has been wired into our psyche since the beginning of time. While there have sadly been some casualties before the inception of I-PRAC, we have now come upon an age where trust is at the helm of direct bookings.

From an emotional standpoint, a psychological standpoint and a commercial standpoint, there is simply no denying the enormous significance of this emotion in the short-term rental space.

You needn't be the next William Shakespeare nor as psychologically enlightened as Freud. But understand that if you are in the business of direct bookings then you are unequivocally in the business of trust, and acquiring trust should be the very first thing on your agenda.

It is impossible to predict what the future holds, as our landscape continues to evolve over time. But one thing that we can claim with absolute conviction is that the future of direct bookings and the future of the ethical growth of our industry is trust.

To find out more about I-PRAC and watch an exclusive video with Chris Maughan, go to **bookdirectblueprint.com**

THE
BOOK DIRECT
BLUEPRINT

Enjoying the book so far?

Leave a review on
Amazon and send proof to
info@boostly.co.uk
for a special (bonus) training!

THE FUTURE OF FURNISHING

HOW TO BUY PRODUCTS FOR YOUR RENTAL LIKE A PRO TO GET A LEG UP IN THE INDUSTRY

MINOAN

Running a successful short-term rental business requires getting a lot of things right. Picking the right property, crunching the right numbers, setting the right prices, finding the right handyperson, getting the right cleaners, taking the right pictures, etc. If you do all the "right" things well, you can build a nice flywheel that turns your rental into an incredibly productive, profitable asset. And, if you can build and implement the right systems, you'll be able to replicate this process over and over again.

As you meet more and more entrepreneurs who have been successful in the short-term rental industry, you'll find one common theme – they are very good at building systems. Systems for picking the right property, systems for crunching the right numbers, systems for setting the right prices, systems for finding the right handyperson, systems for hiring the right cleaners, systems for managing the merchandising of your properties' listing pages (images, copy, descriptions, etc.). Building the right systems is the key.

There's one part of the property management process where we've found a lot of these systems fall short, or simply don't exist at all. The process of ordering *all* the stuff you need for your property before you can go live. You know, bedding, soaps and shampoos, decor, kitchenware, art, furniture – the list goes on.

The reality is what you put IN your property makes a big difference. Often, it is more important than the actual square footage of the property. Don't believe us? Go ahead, look up how much tiny homes are charging a night in vacation destinations. Today's travellers value experiences, thoughtful design and aesthetic more than any previous generation – and it shows in the average daily rate (ADR).

You can look at traditional hospitality as an example of just how far thoughtful furnishing can take you. Luxury hotel groups like Ritz-Carlton or Four Seasons spend a lot more on furnishing than their mid-level counterparts like Marriott or Hilton, even though rooms will have the same square footage. Because of their elevated designs, the luxury hotels are also charging a lot more per night. We're often clear on the value a hot tub, pool, patio, or a tennis court can have on our ADR, but we very rarely think about the role smaller amenities can play. A new coffee maker, an exercise bike, a nice sound system, comfy and chic furniture – the small details can make a large difference in your guest's experience and their appetite to spend.

These things matter. Yet, most hosts overlook them. Understanding the importance of furnishing decisions can completely change the economics of your business. Having a seamless system for selecting, ordering, tracking and managing inventory of products can help you scale more quickly and efficiently when getting new properties up and running.

Here are our tips for furnishing your rental:

1. **Create a project plan.**

Once you've acquired your property, start by making a list of everything you'll need for your property – spoiler alert: it's more than you think! It's easiest to segment these lists by room. Think about each room and its needs – start with furniture and work down to the details: linens, decor and consumables. Give yourself an overall project budget and break up that budget by room, allocating the largest portion for the highest traffic areas: the bedrooms, living room, kitchen and outdoor spaces.

Be mindful about lead times if you're purchasing online. Large items like furniture tend to have longer lead times, smaller items like soap/shampoos and decor tend to have shorter lead times. Order the big stuff first, fill in the smaller details afterwards. If you're a current Minoan member, you can rely on us to help you with these lists.

2. **Balance cost and quality when picking products to set your rental apart.**

Furnishing is all about nailing the balance between products that (1.) look good, (2.) hold up over time, and (3.) are reasonably priced. The most common mistake we see first-time hosts make is that they prioritise number three above numbers one and two. Their bed frames break, their outdoor furniture disintegrates and their plates/mugs shatter every week. They usually learn from their mistakes and operate under "buy nice, or buy twice" after going through the painful realisation that quality does matter.

Tenured hosts know BALANCE is key. They know it's worth spending twice as much for properly treated outdoor furniture that lasts for seven years rather than spend less for wicker furniture that only lasts one season. They know investing in the cool-looking coffee machine that photographs well in the kitchen and will satisfy all coffee lovers will allow them to charge a higher ADR, and that the investment can pay for itself in a few short months. For example, if an elevated coffee bar experience allows you to charge $135 per night, rather than $125, then you're netting an additional $10 per night. If you paid $200 for the coffee maker, it can pay for itself in just twenty nights.

On average, a two-bedroom (2BR) rental furnishing from scratch will need to buy an average of 200 unique items. Having a good understanding of what to buy, what areas to invest more heavily in, and what brands to buy from to balance cost with quality can make all the difference in the world.

3. **Build a system to streamline the ordering, tracking and reordering for replenishables.**

As we mentioned earlier, the average host will buy an average of 200 items for a 2BR rental if they are furnishing from scratch. Historically, they've had to turn to a handful of different suppliers and websites to order everything they need. They'll get beds from one place, mattresses from another, linens from another, soaps/shampoos from another, and so on and so forth. This becomes a bit unwieldy and can be a lot to handle. Tracking budgets becomes difficult. Visibility into order tracking and managing delivery timelines becomes a disaster. You need a single source where you can buy everything you need to get your properties up and running (i.e. furniture, linens, consumables, cleaning supplies, electronics, decor, etc.), while also ensuring product quality.

At Minoan, we believe hosts should never have to pay full retail prices like a traditional consumer. You're running a business, and you should be treated as such by large retailers – more to come on this in a bit. This system is also just as important for replenishment and restocking. What do you do if a guest accidentally damages a chair? How do you track down which one you purchased originally? Go through your emails? What about when you get an email from a guest saying there's no more body wash? Think about inventory, think about ordering and build a reliable system to manage it. This is important at one property but becomes SIGNIFICANTLY more important as you scale to 5, 10, 50, 100, 200+ properties.

There's a unique opportunity hosts have that we see few take advantage of. Most hosts underestimate the VALUE of the special moments happening between people and products in their spaces. In order to really understand this, we need to spend some time inside the brains of the brands and suppliers you buy from.

Let's go there.

Brands/suppliers are focused on a few things:

1. Building good products.
2. Marketing their products to consumers.
3. Getting consumers to buy their products (hopefully many times over).

In today's world, consumers are inundated with options, and brands are fighting to capture their attention, making the conversion from #2 to #3 particularly challenging.

In some cases, brands are spending up to $7 for a CLICK with companies like Google, Facebook, Instagram and Amazon. A click! If a click is worth $7, what's it worth to have guests actually USE their product in a contextually relevant environment over the course of three-to-four days? The answer? It's gotta be worth a hell of a lot more than that.

Let's look at the mattress category as an example. Right now, the average CPC (cost per click) for mattresses is $9.29. This means brands are paying over nine dollars every time someone clicks on their Google shopping ad. You can scroll through images, read a description on a website and scour reviews to try and get a good sense of what the product is like. But, it's hard to tell how good this mattress will actually be at delivering a good night's sleep with just an ad.

Sticking with mattresses as the example, in addition to spending money on ads, a brand's other option would be to consider selling their products to a bricks and mortar retailer, like a Mattress Firm. They would sell to retailers at wholesale pricing, set up the products in a store, and sell to guests at full retail prices. Customers then come into the store, lie on a bare mattress without any sheets or pillows, and wiggle around for two minutes while a salesperson hovers over them – "What do you think!?!?" That also doesn't seem like the best way to see if a mattress will help deliver a good night's sleep.

Let's flip the switch and use your short-term rental properties as an alternative marketing channel for brands. Sleeping on a mattress in your own room, on your own time, for a full eight hours, two or three nights in a row. No salesperson. No ads popping up. Just you and the mattress. Now THAT rich experience will certainly help you see how good the mattress is at delivering a good night's sleep. Those meaningful moments are happening every day in your properties with hundreds and thousands of guests, with hundreds of products – FOR FREE!

At Minoan, we call this "native retail". Using products for exactly what they were designed to be used for, in spaces they were designed to be used in. It's the best possible way for people to try new products before buying. We believe spaces that provide these sorts of rich experiences are the new "four-walled influencers" and they deserve to be treated as such. If this applies to you, you should get significant discounts on products, and you should earn money every time you create a moment of inspiration that leads to a purchase.

That's what most hosts miss. You know you're playing in the experiential economy, but you're missing the equally important opportunity you have in the ATTENTION economy. The one monopolised by Google, Facebook, Instagram, Amazon and others who pay billions of dollars each year on advertising alone.

When you realise this, it completely changes the economics of your business. You no longer view yourselves as "customers" of brands but, instead, see yourselves as a viable marketing partner to help brands reach new potential customers. That shift in perspective has a very different, and much more favourable, economic relationship for you as a host.

Think about how many hotels pay full retail for the stuff they buy for their properties? ZERO. Not a single one. Why? Because brands/suppliers view hotels as strategic business partners to help get their products in front of consumers. With the vacation rental market planning to reach $107B by 2028, brands are beginning to view short-term rentals with a similar lens.

Why am I so passionate about this nuanced topic? Because I've seen the evolution of retail firsthand and how opportune hosts can take advantage. I was an early employee at Jet.com, which went on to sell to Walmart for $3.3B in 2016. I then spent several years at WMT, the largest retailer in the world. Enough time to realise that those moments on screens (ecommerce) and shelves (bricks and mortar) are worth NOTHING compared to the real moments you create every day in your properties. YOU are the new influencer; the four-walled influencer.

It's why we built Minoan. To help you and your properties tap into this value. To make sure you never pay more than you should on mattresses, linens, soaps and shampoos. To help you manage the process of ordering in one place, where you can see delivery dates, budgets, estimated costs, tracking information, etc. Where you can save thousands of dollars buying the things you need, and you can bring these products to life in a digital shoppable experience where you can effortlessly make money off these *moments* of inspiration between people and products.

Minoan can help you fully capitalise on this and change your relationship with brands/suppliers. Here's how:

1. **We easily port products into an immersive digital experience that looks professional and elegant to uplevel the guest experience and give you a way to earn money on the back end.**

   Once you've selected the right products and amenities, you then have to think about how you introduce these to your guests in a way that is "present, but not overwhelming". This part is essential for you to fully capitalise on the richness of the moments you create – but you need to do so in a way that does not NASCAR (overly advertise or label) the space. One elegant, well merchandised site with all products there, broken out by room and by brand, with a bit of unique information about each brand is a great way for guests to discover the products you've hand selected for their stay.

2. **We manage the routing of those orders, customer service, etc.**

This experience needs to also ensure orders get routed to brands, there is ample and strong customer service, and that profit sharing is done automatically on items that have sold. This part is incredibly important, but also challenging for most hosts, as they already have their hands full managing the property and dealing with guests. Managing an entirely different type of business (retail) can often be overwhelming and difficult to maintain at a high service level in tandem with all of the other day-to-day operations related to running a successful short-term rental business. We'll do the heavy lifting, so you don't have to.

3. **We capture data and insights to understand what guests think of products, and a way to port clicks, conversion and customer pathing back to brands without compromising.**

Having this experience sit on an events-based infrastructure so you can capture clicks, conversion, customer pathing and other behavioural data on the site without capturing PII or other personal or identifiable information for guests. As I mentioned earlier, most brand marketers are data-driven now. If you want to earn money (whether in the form of discounts or direct advertising revenue), you need to be able to show them the engagement data they are used to seeing from companies like Facebook and Google. We can help capture and share that information.

I know this is a lot to manage on your own, but hosts who do this well not only save time and money upfront on furnishing, but they also add an ancillary revenue stream to their listing. Through Minoan, for example, hosts can get mattresses averaging 50% off and earn ~10%

commission every time a guest buys one. That means if you get five guests who buy a mattress over the course of a few months, the mattress has already paid for itself. Imagine if every product you put in your property was not just a cost centre, but actually a revenue-generating asset. A mechanism that allows you to continually reinvest in your property with a major economic advantage over other STR vacation managers, owners and operators in your area. That's the competitive edge we can help you build.

At Minoan, we're giving hosts one centralised place to purchase everything they need for their portfolio, across hundreds of high-quality brands like Article, Polywood, Crate & Barrel, West Elm, Wayfair and more. We've negotiated steep discounts for hosts as high as 60% off retail. Minoan helps hosts seamlessly manage reordering for their property to ensure they never run out of stock on essentials. We then build you a best-in-class retail experience you can integrate into your properties and social media channels like Instagram or on direct booking websites, without having to deal with all the unsexy parts (customer service, order routing, etc.).

Whether you're interested in saving money on furnishings, turning your property into a shoppable experience, or both, Minoan will be here to help. Oh, and by the way, did I mention Minoan is completely free?

We strongly believe the intentional coordination of steps 1 – 3 above will, in the eyes of brands and retailers, shift dollars away from the powerful tech giants, and into the hands of people who are creating real, intimate moments of value between people and products. You, the hosts.

To watch an exclusive behind-the-scenes video on how to implement Minoan into your business for free head to **bookdirectblueprint.com**

EFFICIENCY IS THE KEY TO SUCCESS

VINCE BRESLIN – UPLISTING

What is your business goal? Is it a side hustle or do you want to replace your nine-to-five? If you are already running your business, do you want to grow and build a thriving hospitality brand as an operator or do you want a four-hour work week? Do you want to become the next Sonder with 1000s of properties under your belt?

Whichever path you choose, the key to accomplishing your goal is business efficiency. How much can your business produce from the time, money and resources you put into it?

I'm one of the founders of Uplisting, which is software that helps you manage, streamline and grow your short-term rental business. I'll explain more on how Uplisting works in a little bit, but for now I'd like to share how efficiency helps us, a self-funded business, go toe-to-toe with heavily funded competitors. Some of our competitors have raised over $200m!

Although Uplisting is a software business, there are many similarities to building a hospitality business. Each of us is creating something from nothing. Using our skills and experience to make a dent in our market and make our businesses work for us. We're constantly trying to attract our target audience to book (or in our case subscribe to) our product. In the beginning, we have no idea what we're doing, but we keep going, figure it out, and make it happen.

We started with three founders working part-time, evenings and weekends for the first two years of our existence. Sure, a hell of a lot of work and not a lot of social life, but we couldn't have made Uplisting a success without also being efficient. Working smarter not harder, as they say.

Efficiency in Your Target Market

An example of being efficient is focusing on our target market. We focus on growing short-term rental businesses as opposed to someone listing their property on Airbnb as a side business. By doing so, it means we charge a minimum subscription of $100/m. This prices out most side hustles and that's intentional. We experience smaller volumes of customer support, we are guaranteed at least $100/m per account, so can afford to spend on acquisition and we don't have to educate very early beginners on the basics such as how Airbnb works. It's not that we don't want to offer a solution to everyone, it's just not possible for us to do that for many reasons (product requirements are different, we'd need to double our customer support team, etc.).

My co-authors cover the importance of knowing your target audience but it all boils down to being efficient. You can't meet everyone's needs, so focus on those that you can and that will pay for your product.

Get Tech to Do It

One of the best ways to increase efficiency (and your happiness!) is to use software. The way I think of it is this: all repetitive tasks should be done by tech.

At Uplisting, we have built our business on top of various software solutions and use Zapier to connect all that software together. Manual data entry and tasks are kept to a minimum. For example, a bug report is submitted by a member (what we call our users) to our customer support team, our customer support team creates a ticket, this ticket is prioritised and funnelled into Slack, where our technical support team picks it up and solves it. When it's solved, the ticket is automatically sent to the customer support team Slack channel with an update and they then update the member who raised it.

This is efficient, as all data is in one place, and Zapier (the glue between our various software) is used to update the relevant teams when a ticket's status changes. We have over a hundred automated processes just like this.

Processes

Process guidelines or standard operating procedures (SOPs) provide clear-cut directions and instructions on how to go about completing certain processes. When I first saw SOP mentioned, I thought that was something for large enterprises. I was wrong. Every business should have SOPs in place. SOPs allow you to delegate and ensure your business achieves the standards you set.

How to use SOPs to run an efficient business

A common issue with small business operators is the feeling only we can provide the level of service required. It's something only *we* can do properly. Although that's true for some aspects of the business, for the most part it's not.

For example, if a guest complains about something, you may think it's best for you to get involved to solve that problem. But all you're doing is following a few set steps you have in your head.

1. Apologise sincerely.
2. Offer x and y to make it right.
3. If the guest accepts, close the conversation, if not, offer a refund.

This is what an SOP is. Writing down the steps you follow (or recording a Loom video) so that others can take over in your absence. To run an efficient business you can't be stuck in the weeds.

The above is a very basic example, SOPs can have many more steps and conditions.

How you can increase efficiency in your business

If you spend any time manually adding guest email addresses to Mailchimp, for example, get tech to do it. If you update prices and availability on each booking site manually, get tech to do it. If you take direct bookings via email and manually send invoices for payment, get tech to do it.

If you spend too much time stuck in the weeds, prepare SOPs and hire someone to do that work for you. No matter what your goal is, you need to spend your time on adding value (or taking time off!).

Using tech to achieve success

Introduction to Uplisting

I mentioned I'm one of the founders of Uplisting. Uplisting is an Airbnb preferred property and channel manager built specifically for growing short-term rental businesses.

My co-founders, Andy and Tadej, and I met whilst working at an Airbnb competitor in London called Housetrip back in 2015. It was there we discovered the need for a solution like Uplisting firsthand. I spent hundreds of hours talking to hosts, understanding their challenges and needs. Housetrip was acquired by Tripadvisor a year later, so the three of us decided to build our own solution from scratch, and so Uplisting was born. Five years in, Uplisting partners with leading industry experts in the field, including Airbnb, Vrbo, Booking.com, and Google.

Who uses Uplisting?

Uplisting works with a broad range of property managers, from those who manage one or two properties with the ambition of scaling alongside Uplisting, to property managers with thirty-to-forty properties who are looking to cut down costs with Uplisting's flat fee rate, or who are simply looking for a new solution after a previous tech solution failed to meet their needs.

Uplisting also partners with large-scale property managers too – for example, members with 300-400+ properties who previously used traditional software but now want to partner with a platform that can implement changes and upgrades as required, or even build features specifically for their business. Uplisting caters to all types of property managers looking to grow their business, no matter what size, shape, or form.

We've grown with many of our members. Pass The Property, for example, started on Uplisting with seven properties a few years ago, they now manage over 400. I love watching businesses like this grow and succeed and learn a lot from watching them do so.

During recent challenging times, Uplisting powered over $15 million in direct bookings in as little as eleven months! And earlier this year, we secured $300,000 in investments from a simple Twitter exchange with funding, community and mentorship ecosystem, Calm Company Fund. On top of this, Uplisting gives its members the opportunity to invest in the business at any time with an exclusive membership investment scheme, which has led to the company securing a further $200,000.

How Uplisting helps

Uplisting works with property managers to help them scale their businesses in the most reliable and sustainable way possible, through increasing revenue, decreasing inefficiencies, focusing on creating value through a deep understanding of customer challenges and needs, and establishing that all-important five-star guest experience.

For example, updating the availability and pricing on one property on Airbnb is time-consuming. Updating multiple properties on Airbnb, Vrbo, Direct, Booking.com and Google Vacation Rentals accurately is impossible. I mentioned before about using tech to perform as many repetitive tasks as possible. This is a perfect example. Uplisting as the tech does this for you. Update once on Uplisting and Uplisting updates to all booking sites within seconds. Uplisting is faster and makes fewer mistakes.

Another major time-consuming task is messaging guests manually with 'thank you for booking' messages, pre-arrival messages, check-in instructions, during stay messages, check-out instructions, etc.

Automate all of this on Uplisting, whilst keeping the messages personal and relevant to the guest. For example, use their name, check-in date and time and much more with our dynamic message tags.

What about collecting payments for direct bookings, or even going as far as offering payment plans? All automated on Uplisting.

Do you require your guests to sign a rental agreement, pay a deposit, verify their identity? All built-in and automated with Uplisting. We call these pre-arrival tasks and they're a huge help when it comes to direct bookings especially.

Even better, all Uplisting features talk to each other. You can set it up so that your automated check-in message doesn't send unless your guest has signed your rental agreement and/or paid their deposit and/or verified their identity.

Talking about direct bookings, Uplisting provides a click-and-play direct booking website, which is ideal for getting started with direct bookings. When you need something more advanced as you build out your direct booking strategy, Boostly is there to help! Boostly integrates directly with Uplisting to provide an even better direct booking experience.

In summary, Uplisting provides a centralised location featuring the tools and solutions required to efficiently run a short-term rental business, from securely collecting payments to communicating with guests. We make listing on multiple booking sites simple and stress free.

On top of the functions Uplisting provides, we think very carefully about reliability and usability. What good is leaving the work to the tech if the tech isn't reliable? Everything we do is built on top of a reliable foundation. This is one of the reasons Airbnb has chosen us to be a preferred software partner.

We also understand that software needs to be easy to use. We live in a world with high staff turnover. As you scale, you shouldn't need to spend days and weeks training new staff how to use overly complex software. Uplisting is very easy to use.

We find a lot of our members come to Uplisting after working with a solution that has failed to meet their expectations or solve their core challenges.

We care deeply about gaining a deeper understanding of the challenges you face when running your business. Whether that's keeping on top of guest communication, managing cleaning and maintenance, optimising rental listings, establishing prices, or dealing with the dreaded double bookings. We believe your business should be working for you, not the other way round.

The true benefits of property management software and channel management

For those of you who haven't already adopted property management software (PMS), there's no better time than now to get started. Competition is fierce, operational costs of running a business are on the rise with the growing uncertainty of economic stability, and guest expectations are higher than ever. But, how does a PMS support a short-term rental business and what are the benefits?

With a solution like Uplisting in place, property managers have access to the tools they need to streamline their businesses, resulting in cost savings on an operational level and reduced inefficiencies leading to increased profits, happier staff, and more satisfied guests. It's also important to note that tech innovation across the industry has accelerated at an unprecedented rate over the past couple of years, meaning adoption rates have soared. Therefore, installing automated technology in short-term rentals is a must for staying competitive in this lucrative market.

Short-term rental businesses are all entirely unique (think size, brand and scaling goals) and so their requirements are going to differ wildly from one another. That being said, there are a few foundational strategies every property manager should think about implementing. It doesn't matter whether managers are aiming to retain their portfolio or reliably grow, meeting occupancy is always going to be at the top of the priority list.

Demand for short-term rentals is not low. So far this year, we've witnessed a 27% increase in comparison to last year's levels. Put simply, the industry is thriving, as more and more guest personas learn the appeal of alternative bookings. Even business travellers and digital nomads are getting in on the action and benefiting from larger living spaces and home-like amenities. The problem lies in the level of supply. Supply is increasing rapidly with new competitors entering the market every day. In May alone, 88,000 new accommodations were added in the US. So, to get one step ahead, property managers must focus on distribution, visibility and conversion.

So, what does strategic planning look like? Firstly, property managers who've yet to create their own direct booking website should consider the benefits: no nightly fee commission leading to increased profits, a chance to connect with guests and provide a personalised service, which may in turn boost five-star reviews, and overall better representation of the brand. And then there are the benefits of utilising savings made by cutting out the middleman (OTAs), i.e. investing extra profit back into a business for marketing, scaling, or even improving the guest experience.

Up until recently, traditional OTAs largely dominated the travel marketplace. The pandemic, however, revealed an industry need for better cancellation and refund policies. This led short-term rental property managers to seek out new solutions that would enable them to communicate more clearly with their guests and reduce concerns during uncertain times. Attracted by the agility and personalisation options of direct booking sites, managers have begun to use direct booking websites in their marketing strategies.

Our advice to these property managers is to avoid the hassle and wasted time involved in building a direct booking website on their own. Instead, choose an out-of-the-box, click-and-play solution like Uplisting, which guarantees a professional-looking domain, is mobile responsive, has built-in features like customisable payment plans, and can take a direct booking within minutes. Better yet, property managers using this software will benefit from all of our integrated features, including verified guest identification, security deposit collection, and eSign rental agreements. So, just like on traditional OTA listing sites, such as Airbnb, property managers will also benefit from integrated solutions.

Without expert insight, personally created websites can lack the essential elements needed to keep potential bookers engaged and gain conversions. For example, if a direct booking website fails to load pages quickly or is too difficult to navigate, interested parties are going to move on to their next option (i.e. competitor listings). Property managers must remember direct booking websites are competing with OTAs like Airbnb, and so need to be on par with the standards that bookers have become accustomed to.

In terms of creating initial traffic towards a direct booking website, property managers should utilise marketing to previous guests by sending out promotional codes directly to email addresses.

It's also vital to highlight that relying on this solution alone is not enough to boost booking rates. In fact, success in this area is made up of many moving elements, which is why a direct booking strategy should be within an overall marketing strategy. For this reason, Uplisting offers members our expertise as a channel manager with a platform that enables property managers to effortlessly list properties on a range of websites. Why is this important? We've all heard of Airbnb, Booking.com, Vrbo and Google for a reason – these brands are leaders in the hospitality space, they're globally recognised and at the top of their game, meaning travellers naturally gravitate towards them.

Recent research by AirDNA only further highlights the importance of utilising OTA booking websites, with Airbnb sharing their record-breaking Q2 results. After months of increasing guest demand for short-term rentals, the online travel marketplace has confirmed an all-time quarterly high profit made with just shy of 104 million nights booked. For perspective, this is a 25% year-over-year increase (and a 24% increase over pre-pandemic levels).

This is why Uplisting is here to support property managers in all strategic directions, combining direct booking sales with efficiently managed listings across a range of travel markets. Our goal is to help short-term rental businesses reach optimum efficiency and scale in a way that's sustainable and profitable. We believe our automation tech tools and PMS platform with specially selected integrations do just that.

But don't just take our word for it, here's what one of our members, Pass The Property, has to say about our solution: "Uplisting adds a fantastic amount of automation into our business and has allowed us to grow by 750% to over 400 properties." This is a promising statistic for property managers looking to scale their businesses sustainably and reliably in a crowded competitor market.

To watch an exclusive interview with Vince Breslin, the founder of Uplisting, head to **bookdirectblueprint.com**

THE
BOOK DIRECT
BLUEPRINT

Enjoying the book so far?

Leave a review on
Amazon and send proof to
info@boostly.co.uk
for a special (bonus) training!

33 ESSENTIAL TIPS FOR A GREAT DIRECT BOOKING WEBSITE

TOM O'BRIEN – BOOSTLY CTO

Over the past five years, I've seen a huge number of rental property websites. I've also spoken to well over 1000 clients at various stages of building their first or next website and discussed all the things they ever wanted to add to it. There have been good sites and bad sites, beautiful and modern sites, eye-wateringly awful sites. But across all of them, there have always been some commonalities. Things that just work and other things that don't. It's my aim in this chapter to provide you with all the things (in my opinion) that do work! And that every host should aim to include in their direct booking website.

Your website will be the most important employee you can ever hire and one that can always be improved and grow with your business needs. It's an employee that never sleeps, is always happy to help a lead or customer and, best of all, never actually takes a salary. It's like having the best sales team in town working for free. The tricky thing is, at first, they will need some care and attention to help them grow and find their feet. Many businesses seem to not give it the attention it needs on this first hurdle, and I feel their website may never reach its potential to become a non-stop direct booking machine. Wouldn't it be in your best interests to make sure this employee has everything they need to succeed at their job?

I have put together a list of thirty-three of my top tips to build a website that stands out from the crowd and generates bookings effortlessly. I have broken it down into five easy to remember categories:

A) Attention

B) Basics

C) Content

D) Design

E) Experience

A) Attention

So, let's kick things off with attention. You've posted daily on social media linking back to your site, your ads are bringing plenty of eyeballs... but no one is actually booking? With today's dwindling attention span and ever-growing flashy distractions, you need to capture the mind's attention in a split second. If you don't, it's likely they will bounce and never come back. Ouch. Crack this part and the rest will fall into place. Keep them on site and curious for more!

Homepage

The most important page of all, so what is the first thing someone will see when they open your site? Is it enough to entice them to go any further? A photo of a pillow with little more than a business name isn't going to tickle anyone's fancy. A slideshow of your showcase properties and surrounding area, a brief description of how you are going to make my life better by booking with you? Now we're getting somewhere. Tell me more! Tell me what to expect as if I were a five-year-old. Oh, a page full of words, meh, TL;DR (too long, didn't read). Icons and bullet-point sentences with your top highlights, sections broken up with luscious imagery, and a teaser of your best listings? Okay, you got me, I will click here to learn more. I hope you can see just how important your book cover really is and putting in the time and effort to get it right can literally make or break whether people stay longer than two seconds or not.

Chatbot

Ever walked into a shop where one of the staff personally greets you with a friendly smile and asks how they can help? It's nice, right? How can we give a similar experience from a website? Chatbots. If you arrive on a site and are a little lost, chances are you could walk away if not attended. What a chatbot can do is reach out a (robot) helping hand to offer assistance. This can do a couple of things: capture a lead and buy you time to follow up with a human. AI is improving rapidly, and I see bots taking over the internet, just like Skynet said they would, but let's keep it simple in 2022, a simple greeting will do!

Landing Pages

Not everyone walks through the front door of your website. Some may come in from the back. For example, an evergreen ad campaign targeting over fifties at Christmas. What better way to greet them than with content that speaks directly to their wants and desires. Create endless landing pages for every type of avatar.

Lead Capture

I've never been to New York, but it's on my bucket list. I'm sure there is a tonne of things I would love to do, but where to start? I don't even know which neighbourhood would be good to stay in. What's that? You have a guide of the top twenty things to do in New York? Oh perfect, sure I'll give you my email address in exchange for your PDF guide. Easy as that, you just captured a lead. Plug this in to your email software like Mailchimp and you can let me know anytime you have an offer on just the type of places I'm looking for.

Offers

Thanks to my wife, we currently have six giant bottles of shower gel in the bathroom cupboard. Why? Because they were on offer! No sane human can resist a good offer (well, my wife can't, anyway). If you have long-stay discounted rates for the lucky buggers who can actually stay on holiday for a month, or if someone books the log cabin by the lake and you'll throw in two canoes free of charge, make it easy to see and hard to resist.

Awards and Featured

Badges, featured in logos and links are great for credibility. What are you best known for? Not that Tripadvisor certificate of excellence from 2013 that's still stuck in the office window, everyone's got one of those! Your houseboat was featured on the Netflix series 'Stay Here'? Oh yeah, I saw that!

B) Basics

"Fail to prepare, prepare to fail." There are a few things that can be overlooked that will either limit you or put people off before they even get on your site. Building a website is a lot like building a house, it needs a solid foundation laid before we can add on the other thirty-two things mentioned here. Choose the wrong foundation (or worse still, build it on someone else's land) and you will find yourself struggling to get what you imagined. Let's go over the basics!

Platform

Ask 100 web developers which platform is the best and why and you will likely get 100 very different answers. My guess is that around forty of them will say WordPress, as roughly 40% of the internet is running on it. I personally have tried many options, from the easy-to-use Wix and Squarespace, to custom-built solutions like Laravel. I always come back to WordPress. Here's my biggest 'why': flexibility. With so many people using it, there is an endless number of free and cheap tools you can easily add to WordPress to achieve almost anything you can imagine without limitations. Also, at the end of this, try to count how many of these you can apply to your free PMS website…

Domain

If someone asks you, "What is your website address?" can you easily say it in confidence and will they remember it? Or does it need a pen and paper? The easier your domain can be to spell and remember, the better. Don't try to be clever or quirky here. Keep it simple. Also, this should be your actual business name.

Email

While instant booking is great, having other ways to contact you is essential. So, let's keep it professional, as if we are dealing with a real business, not something you are doing in your spare time. Create an email using your domain, e.g. contact@nicestays.com – the best option for me is using Google Workspace. If I am emailing pinkbutterflybarbie85@yahoo.com it doesn't look great.

SSL

Ever noticed that little padlock before the website URL? This lets you know that the website is safe and secure to be entering card details as the site is encrypted. If your site doesn't have this, good luck getting customers! Google will warn anyone away before even opening your site. You can also check the URL to see if it starts with https and not http.

C) Content

So, you have your WordPress site all set up and ready to go, then the dreaded blank canvas hits you... What do I fill the pages with? Let's get into it... Firstly, I highly recommend speaking to your ideal customer avatar. If you don't know who or what that is, then spend some time figuring that out. Are you perfect for family fun holidays with plenty to see and do? Or are you targeting white collar workers flying into the city for a business trip? Knowing this will give your content the focus it needs, creating clear and concise information tailored to your guest.

Text

Let's imagine TikTok users for a moment. If what they see doesn't satisfy them in 0.5 seconds, they scroll on to the next one. If your content can't be easily digested at a glance, then it's a waste of space. Break up big blocks of text with icons, bullet points, shorter sentences. Make it 'scannable' while scrolling. If I have to lean in to focus on a paragraph, it's going to be a TL;DR.

Highlights

Take the text reduction a step further back in time to cavemen drawing on walls that my social media fried brain can understand. Beds, two. Guests, four. Free wi-fi, thank God. Jacuzzi, take my money!

Photos

If you ask me what is the one most important thing above all that can improve a rental website, it would be USE GOOD QUALITY PHOTOS. I used capitals here because I cannot stress it enough. If I am looking for a nice place to stay, I need to see what it looks like in its best light. If you are like me, I will skip ALL other content and go straight to the images. If it looks good, THEN I will read more about it. Still using those grainy pictures you took on your old phone? It ain't gonna cut it. The next guy paid for a professional photographer. The exact same property could either look a million dollars or dollar-store through its photos.

Videos

What's better than photos? If you can, add video! Show me what it's like to be there! Paint the picture in my mind, let me smell the salty sea breeze, feel the sun on my balding head, and taste the margaritas I will be sipping on the ocean-view balcony. Ah yes, I'm there already. Now I can't wait. Book me in.

Reviews

You've been in business for longer than Gen Z have been alive, you've had hundreds of extremely nice reviews over the years, but the first thing people see is that ONE bad one left by that neggy nelly once. Frustratingly, that stain won't come out, even if you ask Tripadvisor nicely. Fortunately, there are review widgets, so you can now automatically pull in reviews from multiple sources, including all OTA listings, Google, Tripadvisor, Trustpilot and more! And the best bit? You can skip the bad ones!

Benefits

"Why should I book on your website and not on Airbnb?" Good question. Here's your chance to grab another win-win. A win for you is not paying 15%+ fees to an OTA. A win for the booker is whatever you want to offer to make it worth their while. The secret here is to make the direct booking a no-brainer while still bagging more profit than an OTA booking. Let's do a quick bit of maths: let's say it's a £2000 booking for a seven-night stay. If they book on Airbnb, you pay £300+ in fees. What can you throw in as a nice gesture that costs you less than £300 that will create a no-brainer benefit? How about a £30 welcome hamper with bread, eggs, milk and bacon? Awesome. Or let's say a one-hour full body massage for two? Heaven. Whatever the deal, as long as it is less of an expense to you than the OTA fee and a far more enticing reason to book direct for the customer, it's a no-brainer win-win.

FAQ

Set some clear house rules with clear answers to frequently asked questions, which might save you some time answering email enquiries with questions such as: Do you accept pets? My two huskies are very well behaved and they never destroy anything in sight when they get bored, promise! Or: I'm planning on bringing my DJ system and fifteen or so mates for a very quiet gathering. It's not a party, promise! Do you accept pets? No. Do you allow parties? No. Simple.

About

Is there something interesting worth sharing about you, your business, your location or properties? Then tell the world! This is your place to shine, let everyone know that you only wash linen with organic fabric conditioner to save the planet, or donate 10% of your profits to the local musical school so they can buy new trumpets. Or that all the furniture in your properties is actually made by your uncle Derek. People love a good story and even better a good cause, so don't be shy.

Blog

Don't let the word 'blog' put you off from writing valuable content. No one wants to read a daily commentary of your day-to-day life in hospitality, but they would love to hear your personal recommendations for what's hot or not in the area. Not only will this help your guests plan the perfect experience while staying with you, but it will also show Google how great you and your website are and that it's worth showing it to more people. Aka, ranking higher through SEO. What experiences can people expect nearby? Change the name "blog" to whatever is appropriate for you.

Management

My grandad always used to say, "If you don't ask, you don't get." If you are looking to scale your portfolio and take on more properties to buy/lease/manage, then make sure you are telling people about it. This could be done on a separate website, but I feel you get a win-win having it on your main booking site while getting more eyeballs on the prize. Bookers who happen to have or know someone who has a property that needs managing will see while booking. Homeowners and landlords will see what a swell job you are doing already on your epic direct booking site and get fomo after seeing the other properties you have in the bag.

Collections

I don't know about you, but I get overwhelmed with choice pretty easily! It takes me longer to make a choice from a restaurant menu than it does to eat the thing. When I'm looking for a place to stay, if I see 100+ options for my search, I'm very likely to give up and ease the headache by cracking open a beer and firing up Netflix instead. My point here is: make it easy. Less brain power required will equal more bookings. Collections are a great way to offer to cut to the chase. Looking for beachfront villas with a pool and a BBQ? CLICK HERE! Child and adult-friendly treehouses in the woods with a hygge vibe? CLICK HERE. Now I only see what I need to see, and I can put the anti-anxiety meds back in the medicine drawer.

Special Occasions

My dog's birthday is coming up soon, it's also the same week as my wedding anniversary. I'd love to make my staycation weekend a little extra special. When I tried to do everything myself last year it was a bit of a disaster. It took hours to blow up the balloons, the ice cream cake melted, and I forgot the candles for the dog's steak. I wonder if the place can help me prepare before I arrive this year to surprise the dog? (And my wife.) I'm sure a great deal of staycations are booked in one shape or form for a special occasion. Birthdays, anniversaries, celebrations of all types. If you are capable of going the extra mile to make a stay a special one, offer it. People will often be more than willing to pay the extra.

Instagram

Empty room photos can be nice, but how about showing some real-world use of that dusty ping pong table from the last family who stayed? The best way to do this is by embedding an Instagram feed and showing all the user-generated content from your guests. This not only looks way more inviting than an empty room as you can actually see people enjoying the spaces, but it shows great social proof that everything is legit and others approve.

Listings

You just tweaked your Airbnb listing description for the twenty-seventh time and it's now perfect. Oh, just need to add that we now have a BBQ and Nespresso coffee machine to the amenities list. Oh, and we have now reduced the mid-week rates. Oh, and we should really add the new photos with the matching curtains and bedsheets. Great, now I only have to add all this to the website, for all thirty listings.

Up until last year, this was just the way things were for updating website listings. Shameless plug coming... We knew there had to be a better solution, so we built it. Three letters for you... API (Application Programming Interface, allowing software to talk to each other). At Boostly, we have built over ten custom PMS (Property Management System) integrations that automatically sync all your listings and keep them up to date with your PMS. Yeah, I know... MAGIC! If you are the person responsible for keeping listings up to date, you will know just how valuable this is. If you aren't, go ask that person :)

API is the future, iCal is the past, Boostly has this now in the present, so give yourself the gift of automation.

D) Design

I could write a whole book about my experience of websites that make me feel seasick if I look at them for too long, so my advice here is: if any of the next four sections are going over your head, leave it to the pros. I think it's great that you put the effort in to building your website yourself, but if it still looks like a child's potato painting at the end, it's not going to do your business any favours. Pay an experienced agency to design and build it for you, it'll be worth it (unless you pay some guy £20 on Fiverr to do it).

Logo

"Can you make the logo bigger?" If you are a designer yourself, you will understand the headache this question causes. If you have asked this question yourself then you have caused a headache. Here's a quick exercise: fire up the laptop and take a quick look on some big-name brands' websites. I'm talking Apple, Nike, Airbnb. How big is their logo? About 1cm wide? Or does it fill a third of your screen?

There's no need for a 4k oil painting logo of your farm-stay with circular calligraphy you can only read when you zoom in. The bigger it is, the more it is like shouting. Let's tone it down, keep it simple. Let the text and photos do the talking.

Fonts

Can you name three fonts that aren't Arial, Helvetica or Comic Sans? If you can, you might have an idea of what a nicer looking modern font looks like. This isn't a Word document. This is the shopfront of your business. The invitation letter to becoming your guest. Basic fonts smells like a basic business. Thoughtful font pairings that express the vibe of your brand shows care and attention to detail, style and class, keeping up with trends. Instead of using Helvetica, try Aktiv Grotesk.

Colours

Believe it or not, colours have a strong effect on our emotions. Blue conveys trust, that's why banks often use it. If you made your whole website lime green because your aunt Edna says it matches the curtains, you could be putting people off within the first glance. If colour isn't your strong point, head over to Pinterest and start a little collection of some eye-friendly colours. Quick tip: keep it soft.

Here's some homework: Google the "60, 30, 10 rule". It's a great way to keep a balance of three main colours. 60% is your primary colour (most often white). 30% is your secondary colour. Try to use a colour from your logo here. And finally, 10% is your accent colour. Think red buttons and icons.

Layout

Okay, take a deep breath... here come ten big words about how to present an appealing website layout:

1. Balance, 2. Contrast, 3. Emphasis, 4. Proportion, 5. Hierarchy, 6. Repetition, 7. Pattern, 8. Space, 9. Movement, 10. Variety.

If you didn't go to design school, you might think this is rocket science. To me, this stuff feels like common sense, but clearly there are a lot of people who don't have it. If it looks or feels off, it is. If you are the type of person who feels uneasy when a picture frame isn't straight, or lines up your cutlery, then you have a good eye for what makes a webpage aesthetically pleasing.

E) Experience

You aren't building the website for yourself, you are building it for your ideal customer. If they can't use it intuitively, then it's going to cause confusion and frustration, ultimately leading to them closing your page pretty quickly. Don't try to reinvent the wheel with any of this. If your kids can't work out how to make a booking, it's too complicated. Nobody reads the manual, even when they get a new microwave. I still don't know what 90% of the buttons do! I just click start. Make booking as easy as clicking start and you won't lose anyone along the way.

Wishlist

I've spent two hours comparing the top ten romantic city escape apartments in Paris to see which ticks all the boxes on my list. View of the Eiffel Tower, check. Walking distance to a café with outdoor seating and sells baguettes, check. But I still can't decide if I like the one with the flowery wallpaper bedroom or the one with the flowery sofa more. If only there was a way to save my favourites, so that I can easily come back and make the final decision after sleeping on it for three days. Wishlists!

Search/Map

How far away is the pub? I'll show you! If a picture tells a thousand words, then a map must tell even more. Bookers can clearly see your property is a stone's throw away from the beach and there's a café down the road where they can get a good fry up for breakfast in the morning.

Contact

Hopefully you don't need to hit the '4' button twice and then three times just to type 'Hi' on your phone! If your phone is smart enough to know Snake was fun twenty years ago, then I believe the easiest step you can take to increase the number of booking enquiries is to add text messaging to your website. WhatsApp is the go-to for our side of the planet, but go with whatever works for you. If guests are finding it hard to choose between the tepee or the yurt and want your opinion which will be warmer so Granny doesn't freeze her socks off at night, let them ask you straight away and advise they book the yurt.

Rates and Availability

Imagine the disappointment after spending hours searching for the perfect place to stay on holiday to be told something like, "Sorry, that price on our website is outdated, it's actually £X." OR, "Sorry, we don't have availability on those dates." Bummer. If your website isn't showing live up-to-date pricing and availability then your site is just a tease. If you are still updating these manually after every booking you pencil in your diary, then it's time for an upgrade. By integrating your website to your PMS via API, every time someone searches your sites, they will always be seeing accurate details without you lifting a finger.

Hidden Pages

So, the WiFi password is X$4?2#Z% and the door code is 285639, got that? Not to worry! The house rules and guidebook are all on our website and the secret link will be sent to you in your booking details. Not all pages on your website have to be public or accessible from the navigation. Some you can keep private only for your guests.

As you can imagine, some things are easier to show than tell, so let me show some live examples of all the above to get your creative juices flowing! Head over to **bookdirectblueprint.com** so I can show you more.

THE
BOOK DIRECT
BLUEPRINT

Enjoying the book so far?

Leave a review on
Amazon and send proof to
info@boostly.co.uk
for a special (bonus) training!

REVENUE MANAGEMENT STRATEGIES TO BOOST YOUR DIRECT BOOKINGS

PRICELABS

Revenue management is the art and science of "who to sell, when to sell, how to sell and what price" to ensure that your properties make sustainable revenue that drives a profitable business. Even if you don't know you're doing it, the very act of putting your short-term rental up for booking on any booking channel (direct, or through an OTA) requires you to decide what price to list at – that itself is an act of revenue management.

Any time you fluctuate your prices up or down based on season, for a big holiday, or add last minute discounts, you're practising revenue management.

A lot of focus within revenue management in our industry goes to "what price", and we'll dive into its importance to your book direct strategy shortly. But the other three – who to sell, when to sell, how to sell – are equally important.

Book direct is a revenue management strategy in itself

"How to sell" is particularly relevant to a discussion on direct bookings, as choosing to do more direct bookings is in fact a revenue management strategy, even if you didn't think of it as one. You are looking to diversify your distribution and add another source of demand to ensure you have a sustainable business. This is precisely what the "how to sell" is for.

This is such an important but complex part of a hospitality business that large hotel chains also struggle with it. Their revenue teams change distribution strategy to ensure that they aren't too reliant on a single OTA, and as many guests book direct. Their marketing teams offer loyalty programs that come with perks (free upgrades, better cancellation policies) that might not be available to those who book via the OTAs.

If you're reading this book, you probably know why direct bookings are more cost-effective than bookings from other channels and, in the long run, less risky as you're in control of your listing more than when it's dependent on the OTAs. However, without proper revenue management strategies, the profit could be a myth.

"Who to sell", "when to sell" and "at what price" are important considerations for direct bookings, and we will dive into strategies around that later in this chapter. Together they form a powerful toolbox – dynamic pricing and stay restrictions – that's important to understand.

Overview of dynamic pricing and stay restrictions as revenue management tools

Demand ebbs and flows – the easiest example most of us in the industry understand is high and low seasons. If you set similar prices in Feb and Aug for a beach vacation home in Cannes, you'll either have an empty Feb, or sell-out Aug at a fraction of what you could have made in summer.

Similarly, day of the week fluctuations, big holidays and events that drive abnormal demand should result in different prices, so you attract consistent bookings at a price point that makes it profitable to run your business. We do want to be careful – wanting consistent bookings doesn't mean aiming for 100% occupancy – that indicates that you were underpriced. In fact, the high season in many markets helps offset the costs for the low season when demand is low. You want to make sure that you aren't underpriced there.

Prices should also fluctuate based on how far out a date is. If it is a year out, you might not be in a hurry to sell those nights. If it's next week, you run the risk of those nights sitting empty and might offer some last-minute discounts. This is the "when to sell" part, and is especially important for direct bookings.

Lastly, when the high season is far out, and there's plenty of demand left, you can be choosy about only wanting to take longer bookings. Going back to the Cannes example, a lot of weekend bookings in Aug would mean you have a scattered calendar with plenty of open days midweek. You'd rather take week-long bookings if you can get them, and then fill the remaining gaps with shorter bookings. This is "who to sell", and dynamic stay restrictions in short-term rentals create a unique filter for the type of stay you are willing to take.

The above factors, namely seasonality, day of week, events/holidays and booking window (far out vs close in) are what we call "proactive" strategies. There's also a set of "reactive" strategies that depend on the state of your calendar. For example, you might not be open to short two or three-night stays in peak season, but what if you get two seven-night bookings with a three-night gap in between? If you continue with your minimum stay requirement of seven nights, those three nights are going to stay vacant. Given the current state of your calendar, you might take a reactive approach and reduce the minimum stay to three nights, resulting in better revenue possibilities.

Another reactive strategy is called pacing, where you try to gauge how well you're doing against the same time last year, or against the market. For example, if the high season is two months away, and the market is almost booked out, and you were fairly well booked last year but aren't this year, you're "pacing behind" the market. It might be time to reduce your prices and stay restrictions because something is making guests not book you (maybe the market is going through a downturn, maybe your expectations from the year were higher than before and you raised rates).

The section above provided a broad overview of basic revenue management principles that apply regardless of whether you're selling on the OTAs or on your direct channel. It is important to be aware of and master these strategies for the overall health of your business.

The sections below will explore some practical strategies that you can apply to drive profitable direct bookings. The focus there is not overall revenue management strategies, but specific ones.

Revenue management for book direct: cost considerations

We all commonly understand that direct bookings is a cost-effective channel and want it to become an important pillar for our independent business. While we strive to improve our direct bookings, it is important to remember that direct bookings should stay at least as profitable as OTA bookings for it to be a successful ongoing strategy.

This requires a close look at your business metric. To drive direct bookings to your short-term rentals, you spend on technology, marketing, or time (yes, it's money) – do you have a sound grasp on these and are certain the costs don't exceed the savings on OTA commission? You should factor in every cost that's involved in making your direct booking channel successful and compare it head-to-head with your OTA commissions.

Would high costs mean driving direct bookings is too complicated and you shouldn't do it? No! Absolutely not. There are some easy tactics that can help you drive direct booking as a channel and reduce your total cost of operations!

Understand the cost of your book direct channel. Repeat after me – I will make sure to understand the cost of my direct booking channel fully. This could include:

a. Your technology costs: these include the property management system (PMS) and direct booking website (without these, your direct booking strategy can't be online, which in today's age won't take you very far).

b. Your marketing spends: any technology you use to capture guest emails, software subscriptions you use to send out offers to them, any social media advertisements you run.

c. Your time spent: this one is hard to quantify, but time you spend on activities specifically around book direct marketing doesn't come for free – you could have been doing maintenance work around the house (that you ended up hiring someone for), or working on message automation via your PMS.

d. Consultant salaries: depending on how tech-savvy you are, there might be times you hire a consultant to set up systems for you to operate later on. If you're all about DIY, then consider yourself that consultant and chalk up the cost in the "your time spent" category!

An understanding of your channel costs is extremely important for you to make decisions about some of the tactics described below. The great thing about book direct is that, unlike OTAs, where the costs are constant, on book direct a lot of the costs are up front, making it riskier, but the ongoing costs can be significantly lower, making it a lot more rewarding in the long run.

The tactics below assume you have established that direct book can be a good channel for you, and you have spent time with websites, social media, ads, etc. to drive traffic.

Key Revenue Management Tactics to Consider

Rate parity

Suppose your prices across an OTA and your direct website are the same but on the OTA the service fee is charged on top. The revenue you make on a booking from either channel (OTA or direct) is the same. But the service fee on the OTA was on top of the revenue you made (the guest paid that marketing fee), and on book direct, the costs are being paid from the revenue you made – effectively, you are left with lesser money. This is fine if you are okay with losing some profitability to drive direct bookings as a stronger channel in the beginning, but once you have a steady book direct flow, you can start bringing the final price a guest pays to be closer to the OTA prices.

You might evaluate that if your marketing expenses are not as high as the commissions OTAs charge, then you can price things so that you and your guests split the marketing fee (they get a deal by booking direct, and you get more than if they'd booked via an OTA). But it is important that this is a conscious choice.

From a trust perspective, it is also important to have the price on your direct booking website not be a total steal – savvy guests are wary of online scams, and your place being very cheap doesn't help build confidence.

Repeat booking next year

You go out of your way to make your guests feel welcomed and they can be the best source of business for you. There are plenty of guests who would want to book their next holiday with you while they're wrapping up their current stay. There are a few simple things to think about for these guests: availability, minimum length of stay and price.

Availability: You expect a guest who's staying with you to check with you about availability next year. But many might just go to your direct booking website (hopefully by now you've communicated about the direct booking website – if not, they might just return via the OTA). Making sure your calendar is open to taking bookings fourteen-to-eighteen months out ensures that the guests are able to find enough dates next year and book something!

Minimum LOS: Although you want the returning guests to book next year, you don't want them to book a short three-night stay right in the middle of your busy season when you're mostly expecting seven or more night stays. In addition to availability, make sure you have your restrictions also set up, so you only take bookings you want to.

Price: We often come across hosts who let guests book their properties for next year at the same price as the current year, or sometimes even lower, citing "early bird" discounts. However, this may not always be sound. What if, without realising, you were undercharging this year, should that inadvertent discount continue next year too? Or maybe there are special events or sudden popularity for your area. Or the most mundane of all reasons – inflation! Even if nothing else is happening, prices for most things next year will go up, and your guests understand this! Don't leave that money on the table by letting someone book early and at the same price as last year.

Before offering a booking for the next year, look at how your current year's bookings compare to other bookings in the market. Several market data tools can help you understand this directionally. If the rates were fine, allow the current guests to book early but at a slight premium. The thing to consider here is that you must believe that they enjoyed the stay at your property and that costs increase over time. Some premiums should be explainable.

Stimulating demand during low season

We touched upon guests who want to repeat their amazing vacation next year. But from a revenue management perspective, the true success story is if you can get a repeat guest to book during low or shoulder season. That's when you have plenty of availability that you're not sure of getting a booking on. That's precisely where creating a mailing list and marketing former guests with offers to book directly with you can come in handy. This marketing can result in "stimulating demand" that didn't exist before.

We earlier talked about how during the high season you don't want to discount rates for your guests. The story flips a little during low season when you have plenty of availability. These nights would potentially go empty and not generate any revenue. In such cases, you won't be mistaken to try and nudge your former guests into booking a weekend out on budget.

Do note that most guests are savvy about money and might search up OTAs before booking your place. Generally, it's better to maintain rate parity (final amount that guests would pay) across your booking channels, including direct book, and offer some discount coupon at the end. It should make it easier for your tech stack as well.

Instead of making it about a discount, you can also make it about exclusive amenities that are only available via your direct book channel. When it comes to amenities, you can also think of some amenities that are not available via traditional booking channels but can be bought only via your direct book channel. Coupons to a local vendor (who is also experiencing their low season), early check-in/late checkouts, etc. can all help!

Using the "trust" to take bookings you won't take via an OTA

Like most short-term rental operators, you probably have a list of red-flag bookings that you avoid. These can be weekend bookings to locals, single night bookings, and more.

However, once a guest has stayed with you, knowing what you know about them, you might be more willing to accommodate their special needs. Maybe if you know the family, you'll be okay with booking a one-night transit stay on the way to the airport, knowing that they're not going to trash your place. Do ensure that you don't do this while putting your revenue at risk – a one-night mid-week booking during low season is okay, but during high season it jeopardises your potential revenue from dates around it.

Seasonality or special events

We talked early on in this chapter about how demand ebbs and flows, and how adjusting prices for seasons, holidays, different days of the week, etc. is extremely important, not just on your direct booking website, but on any OTA. Many OTAs also offer price recommendations taking this into account, but it's important to not allow those to adjust prices on the OTA directly as it'll go against the rate parity discussion we had earlier. You might end up selling on that OTA at a very different price from the direct booking website.

So, what can you do? Thankfully, there are many solutions available. For one, if you've been in business for more than a year, your own data might show you booking patterns for various seasons (for example, high season generally tends to book earlier compared to low season, especially if you didn't raise rates for it compared to the low season). You can also dig into your data to see if weekends were more popular and by how much, which can guide you to increase rates accordingly. There's a lot of economics that can go into this, but as an easily implementable rule of thumb, if weekends had an occupancy rate 20% higher than the weekdays, then they should be at least 20% more expensive than weekdays. Outside of your own historic data, there are plenty of market data providers out there that can guide you.

On the marketing front, we've talked about how your marketing list can come in handy during low season when you're not getting enough demand from the OTAs. But that list can also come in handy when you're headed into your high season. Are there high seasons or special events in your area that are bound to get booked? Can you drive traffic for those days to your book direct channel?

If you expect a day to have very high occupancies, why bear high channel costs for those days? You should open those days on your low-cost channel – direct book. Your book direct channel should be easy to find and mature enough to trust because guests are unlikely to book a high-cost stay if the process isn't seamless and trustworthy.

Many large vacation rental companies double down their focus on direct bookings during their high season precisely because OTA commissions can add up to a lot during this time. However, they are in a position to do so only because they've been in business for a long time, and have a sound and well-established book direct strategy. This isn't something we'd recommend for smaller companies that don't have all the wheels of book direct in motion already.

Conclusion

We've talked about a lot in this chapter, from general revenue management strategies as well as those specifically applying to book direct. It is important to understand that one doesn't work without the other.

But more importantly, it is important to realise that revenue management is one of the many spokes in the direct booking wheel – having a good marketing strategy, seamless book direct website and prompt guest communication are all what will eventually lead to guests trusting your website and clicking that "Book" button. Understanding that most guests will do many searches on OTAs before clicking that "Book" button to see if your place is cheaper elsewhere, or if another similar place is available, is probably the most important revenue management principle.

Once you've convinced someone to take a vacation in low season through your marketing efforts, you don't want them to book elsewhere.

To find out more about Pricelabs head to **bookdirectblueprint.com**

INCREASE CUSTOMER LOYALTY BY ELEVATING THE GUEST EXPERIENCE

DACK

"It's just that great isn't good enough anymore. It's how you look at your business...and how customers see the difference, if any, between you and the competition."
McKain 29

In an increasingly crowded market, with the demands of travellers changing, conversations in our industry are increasingly centring around how vacation and short-term rental operators can stay both competitive and relevant. It is no longer enough to provide exceptional service, communication, and a top-notch property. Now, a relentless focus and attention to the entire guest experience is the path to success for short-term rental operators. If a hospitality operator facilitates a memorable experience for their guests, above and beyond the expected reliable service, they will stand apart from the crowded competitive field.

In most cases, the booking of a short-term rental is a routine transaction at *the end* of a selection process. When the customer has decided on a destination, a property and a schedule, the booking completes the process. On their own, the customer might continue to research the destination and envision the coming trip, but in most cases, the short-term rental operator plays little to no role in this effort. What if, instead, the booking is regarded not as an end but as *a beginning*. The booking opens an opportunity for engaging with the customer, and assisting them in shaping the trip that is ahead of them. After the "Book Now" button has been clicked, your guest starts to imagine what their trip might look like. What kinds of activities are available? What are the best restaurants? What are the not-to-miss tourist attractions? What they expect is to search the internet, sorting through myriad options and reviews, overwhelmed by the results and at the mercy of advertising and SEO. Too often, there is no connection between the booking the client has made and the experience they hope to have.

Generating a connection between a booking and the experience opens the door for a vital, and mostly neglected, opportunity for value creation that benefits guests AND operators. When the host steps in at booking and provides a curated, personalised set of recommendations and opportunities to their guest, this transforms a routine transaction into the start of a memorable experience that will be associated with the hospitality company and their distinct brand and personality. By sharing insider knowledge, guiding choices and offering exclusivity, a mundane and sometimes stressful activity becomes next-level.

Of course, five-star hotels and resorts have always recognised – and built their brands on – this insight. The MVPs (minimum viable product) of those hospitality teams are the concierges that satisfy high-end guests by facilitating their requests, and delight these same guests by presenting them with opportunities that they didn't even know they wanted until they were offered. These large hospitality brands have prioritised their commitment to an exemplary guest experience to the degree that they have spent billions – yes, billions! – on technology to meet the needs of today's customers.

Offering this kind of personalised service to every guest can be costly, and might sound inefficient, and possibly downright impossible for the already busy short-term rental operator. You might be thinking that you already have a recommendation section on your website, or offer links to local activities in your automated emails. Isn't this enough? Maybe, if your goal is to simply facilitate booking nights in your rental property. But if you want to drive engagement with your brand that will turn a one-time guest into a repeat customer, you will need to create a memory, not simply provide a service. As B. Joseph Pine II and James Gilmore assert in *The Experience Economy*, "… services are about time well saved, while experiences are about time well spent." (p13)

How can you create this unique guest experience? By creating a place where your guests can, through your curated choices, shape in advance the time they will spend with you. In fact, according to Google consumer research, 67% of travellers are more loyal to a hospitality company that provides them with opportunities to enhance their experience during their stay.

For the short-term rental operator, this place is DACK, a revolutionary product built with a focus on the guest – one app, one solution, one flow. Your hospitality company will be able to step in and provide unique, personalised value to your guests at scale. And not only can you accomplish this at a fraction of the cost of creating your own technology, DACK will boost your revenue beyond the nightly rate, adding to rather than subtracting from your bottom line. Supported by a robust back-end platform with enough flexibility to work with your existing tech configuration, DACK will enable you to provide a remarkable, differentiated, guest-centric journey on the technology platform your customer prefers: their phone.

DACK is not just a "digital guidebook". Digital guidebooks lack the in-app interactivity, the opportunity for connection and engagement between operator and guest, that will keep your company at the top of a traveller's mind the next time they're booking a getaway. DACK is an experience platform, more concierge than guidebook, with powerful ecommerce capabilities and strategic partnerships that create opportunities to not only wow your guests, but generate revenue, improve reviews, and drive more direct bookings.

Utilising the DACK app, vacation rental operators of all sizes can compete on the same level as the most distinctive luxury brands without the investment required to build their own technology. DACK provides opportunities for differentiation and customisation that can turn a service into an experience, creating sticky memories that will turn one-time guests into loyal brand advocates. We help operators shift from a service to an experience mindset that creates more value for their guests, and as a result, more revenue, more loyalty, more direct bookings and less dependence on online travel agencies (OTAs).

In Pine and Gilmore's *The Experience Economy*, the authors describe two essential elements for successful customisation at scale, "… a *design tool* that matches customer needs with company capabilities and a *designed interaction*, within which a company stages a design experience that helps customers decide exactly what they want." (p 135) The DACK platform enables you to expand your capabilities to design the ultimate guest experience, creating a personal relationship with your guests while giving them the autonomy to select from meaningful choices at their leisure.

How does this magic happen? How do you walk your guests through this journey that will elevate their experience, gain efficiency and revenue for your business, and convert them into repeat, direct bookers? The answer is *experience mapping*, and the platform is DACK. Let's dig in…

First developed by Conifer Research, a marketing firm that helps "align business decisions around the lives and needs of real people", a 5E Experience Map can give you, as a host, the framework to design a guest-first journey that, when used in conjunction with a platform like DACK, creates an engaging, repeatable and scalable journey that builds loyalty and trust. We strategise around these five stages – entice, enter, engage, exit and extend – with our clients to enable them to successfully execute a high quality mobile experience for their guests.

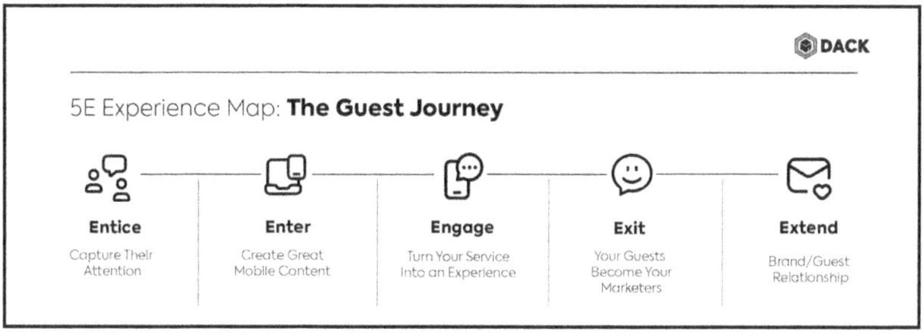

Entice

> "Hospitality is present when something happens for you. It is absent when something happens to you. Those two prepositions – for and to – express it all."
> Meyer, 10

You have a new booking. Perhaps this reservation is from Airbnb or another OTA, or perhaps it's a first-time guest that found your company as they were researching their location. You have some options here. You could send them a booking confirmation, and maybe a string of emails and text messages with recommendations. Assuming that they read their emails and clicked on links you've provided about their destination, you've now sent them to the internet, where an overwhelming array of options await. Or, maybe you leave it to them to figure out how they want to spend their time, and they have an amazing experience on their trip. That's great, but your guest is not going to attribute any of this success to you, the hospitality operator. This is most likely your guest's regular experience, one they usually get from other hospitality companies, and expect to get again. If you proceed this way, you live up to your guest's *expectations*, and provide a satisfactory *service*. However, you are probably indistinguishable from your competition and you have given your guests no reason to think much about you or your brand.

With guest technology like DACK, you proceed in a different way after booking. You entice your guest to follow your lead, capturing their attention and piquing their curiosity. You communicate that you have specifically considered their needs and possible interests, and have a unique offering for them. You let them know that you have a personalised app, designed with their trip in mind, curated with your favourite experiences and local recommendations. You remind them of the real people making these suggestions, community members that have knowledge of the destination and a stake in the success of their holiday. You have given them a resource that is free from bots, SEO and affiliate marketing, saved them from an overwhelming experience on Tripadvisor or Time Out. You have created a tool to save them time and trouble because, as an exceptional host, the quality of their experience is your top priority.

With an over 70% app registration rate, with some operators reaching upwards of 130% (via invitations to other members of the party), we can confidently say our operators are succeeding at enticing their guests.

Enter

"The modern consumer doesn't reward passable experiences – they want to be dazzled every time they interact with a brand. When it comes down to it, we're all in the business of wooing our customers with a stellar experience."
Brandwatch

It's all about first impressions, right? You've spent time creating inviting spaces, compelling listings, and excellent photos to encourage guests to choose your company or your property over the competition. The DACK app is an extension of that experience, further reassurance to your guest that they have selected wisely. And through modern and forward-thinking product design, we've made sure that the app is easy to navigate, a remarkable experience in and of itself. Organised into clear sections, your guest knows at a glance that this is their one stop to plan their stay. And with design tools and a user-friendly interface built into the back-end operator portal, we make it easy for you to create high-end content, easily customised to reflect your distinct brand identity.

Why is this important? For the guest, no more digging through emails, or searching for the FAQ section on your website. With one click into the DACK app, your guests have all the information they need for an exceptional stay at their fingertips. This is your front desk, your opportunity to greet your guest and introduce your brand. The future of check-in, you've gone beyond just "contactless" and, instead, have provided a comprehensive resource. And for you? After investing a small amount of time in a well-designed guest app, you'll have fewer phone calls and emails, increased efficiency, and many more informed, happy, impressed guests.

Engage

"Today's consumers are not the consumers of yesterday. They are more resourceful, selective, technological, and accustomed to convenience... if you don't offer what your customers value, someone else will – and you'll lose your customers to competition. But if you can begin by messaging, personalizing, reducing friction, increasing convenience, and improving customer experiences with technology, you'll convert customers for life."
Podium

You have the attention of your guest, giving you a unique opportunity to build the relationship. Like a best-in-class concierge, you can show your guest you've anticipated their needs before they have to ask. You have customised a service, turning it into an experience. They could have booked with that other company, but they booked with you. And you have a platform to engage them long before they arrive at their property, to offer them a unique, unforgettable experience. Through a variety of well-timed and well-crafted notifications, you continuously bring them back into the app, serving as their trusted guide. With technology we all use every day, you are forming a personal connection.

You've put yourself in your guest's shoes, and thought through every question they might have in preparation for their journey. Your amenities are detailed, your property guide well thought out. You've outlined their check-in instructions, eliminating day-of-travel stress. You've compiled your list of your favourite local restaurants, cafés, off-the-beaten path destinations that won't be found on tourism websites. You've divided these into clear categories so they can easily find what they're looking for: Family Friendly, For the Adventurous, Breakfast Spots, Midnight Snacks. (I'm staying with one of our customers soon and was instantly intrigued by the Speakeasy category on their app.) And you've encouraged them to invite the rest of their party to the app, giving everyone a chance to participate, extending your relationship beyond the primary booker.

Within the DACK app, we've provided an ecommerce platform for you and other experience partners to offer guests ways to enhance their stay. Putting the ecommerce in the app allows you to curate what the guests are offered, and it helps ensure that the guests will also associate those offerings with you, their host. Our platform lets you give guests the opportunity to opt in to the activities and services that interest them, with the ease of online shopping we've all become accustomed to. Whether a standard offering like early check-in or cleaning services, luxury concierge services like private chefs or transportation, or local tours and activities provided through our partners or your own, your guest can create an experience tailored to their individual preferences.

Exit

"Word of mouth is more effective than traditional advertising for two key reasons. First, it's more persuasive... Second, word of mouth is more

targeted. It is naturally directed towards an interested audience...But want to know the best thing about word of mouth? It's available to everyone. And it doesn't require millions of dollars spent on advertising. It just requires getting people to talk."
Berger, pp. 8-9

Because you've taken into consideration how your guest feels every step of the way, provided them with quality options for the best possible holiday and created a space where they experienced value and felt valued, they are going home on a high emotional note. They've had an amazing experience and their fellow travellers are also raving about what a great time they all had. And what do people do when they've experienced something extraordinary? They share. They share via social media, they share via text messages to their family, they share at work when coworkers ask how their trip was, they share the next time they're out with friends. And because you, the exceptional host that you are, guided them every step of the way and provided them with your own easy-to-use technology, what are they unlikely to say when asked where they stayed? "At an Airbnb." "At a place I found on Vrbo." They will proudly tell everyone about you, this fantastic hospitality company they discovered, and all of the ways you helped them create exactly the type of trip they were hoping for.

Your guests will do your marketing for you, lead other potential guests to your website, and garner more direct bookings, at no additional cost to you.

Extend

If you've done your part, strategically utilised the tools available within the DACK app and your own local network, provided an extraordinary experience to your guest, complemented with a high level of customer service, you will see results. According to a 2019 study by Medallia and Ipsos surveying customers, "77% claim to have chosen a product or service from a company because of good experiences they had with it."

And isn't that what we're here to talk about? Through the use of a *designed tool* (DACK) in combination with a *designed interaction* (your customisation of the guest experience), you will see an increase in rebookings, directly through your website, widening your audience of loyal guests, and decreasing your cost of guest acquistion.

And there's more good news. In the same study, Medallia found that 73% of customers are willing to pay higher rates because of a good experience. That's right – not only can you increase your ancillary revenue through DACK's ecommerce platform, and not only will your high-end service lead to more direct bookings, saving you money – you will be positioned to capture a higher nightly rate than your competitors. Take a look at this chart from Pine and Gilmore's *Experience Economy*. Utilising DACK's platform, you're customising your service, delivering it elegantly via a guest app, and providing a differentiated experience tailored to your customers.

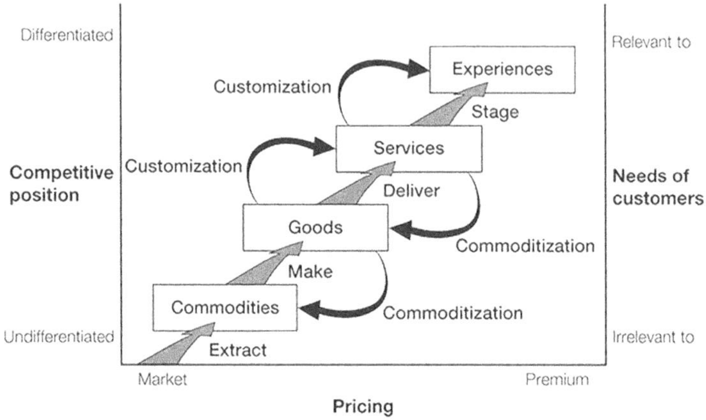

The Progression of Economic Value, from Pine and Gilmore's *Experience Economy*

Of course, our position isn't that technology should replace human connection. After all, the Oxford Dictionary's definition of hospitality is a "friendly and generous behaviour towards guests." Instead, we view the app as an extension of this connection. Your guests will appreciate the convenience and efficiency of a mobile platform to find the answers to their questions or peruse at their leisure the itineraries you've created for them. In combination with an effective engagement strategy, a guest app provides a much better option over endless emails, and an ecommerce platform with automations is a clear advantage for your guests and your operations team.

Think about the last time you travelled with an airline or booked with a hotel. I don't know about you, but searching through my jumbled inbox trying to locate reservation information is a chore. Trying to relocate a weblink to find an answer to a simple question is a headache. If I need to call or email to request a simple upgrade like early check-in, I feel frustrated (especially knowing that "there's an app for that!"). But simply logging into a travel app, where I'll find all the information I need, in advance of my departure? Or going through a simple online payment process when I have an opportunity to enhance my stay? It's a pleasure, and based on the reports of increased revenue and efficiency that our customers report, it's clear that their guests think so too.

I mentioned earlier that I have an upcoming reservation with one of our customers, giving me the opportunity to use their app as a guest. Clearly, it's hard for me to be entirely objective. However, I have fallen in love with our product all over again. I've been delighted by every push notification reminding me of my upcoming adventure, bringing me back into their impeccably designed app. I've clicked through all of their extremely fun and hyper-local recommendations, giving me a chance to make my plans in advance. I've looked through their check-in instructions and amenities, a great guide as I prepare to pack. I have purchased early check-in with the click of a button. I am a happy guest, and if I close my eyes and pretend I know nothing of DACK, I can honestly say that the host's attention to my needs would put their company at the top of my list the next time I have a chance to visit their destination.

And our customers report that the experiences of their guests match mine. Beyond simply the convenience of property and access, and the ease of choosing from options to enhance a stay, their guests are simply having fun. Engaging with the app to explore and plan, they are daydreaming about their vacation that they booked months in advance.

Connecting your guests directly to your brand, providing them with next-level service in the palm of their hands, helping them create memories that they'll associate with you: the right technology will turn one-time guests into loyal customers, direct bookers and brand advocates who will spread the word about your exemplary hospitality. The flexibility and accessibility of the DACK app will allow you to facilitate a curated journey that starts with the booking and the anticipation of the trip, unfolds through the stay itself, and remains in mind as your guests begin to think about their next travel opportunity. And they'll be thinking, "I wish every vacation rental company had an app like this," proving that you've differentiated yourself from the competition. Circling back to the quote that started this chapter: "It's just that great isn't good enough anymore." It's time to aim for the extraordinary, a step up from the status quo.

To see an exclusive video from the team at DACK go to **bookdirectblueprint.com**

THE DIRECT BOOKING MOVEMENT IS A WEB3 MOVEMENT

DTRAVEL

Throughout history, disruptive technologies have redistributed ownership and control away from archaic establishments or systems and into the hands of those who are willing to embrace change. In fact, we don't need to venture very far back in time to examine a few relevant examples.

Up until the 21st century, the conventional way of bringing a physical good to market was to find a manufacturer, start a trade show circuit and attempt to get your product onto the shelves of a distributor who earns a margin for selling it to the end customer. Not only did you lose out on building valuable relationships with your customers, but also a part of your profits while taking the majority of the risk.

It wasn't until 2006, when, after attempting to sell snowboard equipment online, Tobias Lütke and Scott Lake built an alternative to the traditional retail model by founding Shopify. This technological shift ultimately lowered the barrier to entry for businesses, empowering them to sell directly to customers across the globe at a fraction of the cost.

Businesses like Shopify have been essential for disruptive innovation that has disintermediated value chains, such as those between sellers of goods and their customers.

However, as these platforms have created this value, they have become too large and centralised, ultimately forgetting about the needs of their users at the expense of the need to earn profits.

The result is that businesses have little say in the direction of the platforms in which they participate, and they are highly dependent on them.

Despite the disruptive innovation, today's ecommerce businesses have little say in the future direction of the infrastructure they use and are still reliant on not only the platforms in which their stores are hosted, but the payment processors that govern each transaction.

Similarly, traditional services like home sharing originated as a direct relationship between a host and guest, but with the advent of online travel agencies (OTAs) and third-party booking platforms, though they've enabled ease and innovation, control and ownership have been taken away from the hospitality providers.

Over the last few years, we've witnessed a movement rapidly gaining momentum that will be supercharged by new technology – the direct stays movement and the emergence of web3. These trends, which share many similarities in their end goal, are on a collision course that will unequivocally revolutionise the future of travel.

The future of direct bookings is web3.

Direct Bookings, a Business as Old as Time

The 2010s saw the rise of the sharing economy – an economy where two parties transact in a peer-to-peer manner and share goods and resources – in various industries, such as transportation, accommodation and item rentals. While companies like Airbnb and Vrbo are credited with the innovation of the home-sharing economy, home sharing and direct bookings have been around for some time.

Homestays

The original concept of home sharing has its roots in homestays. A homestay is a type of accommodation that provides guests with an empty room and meals in a host's home, with an authentic experience of living amongst the host family and experiencing the daily life and culture of the local family. Homestays were primarily used by students attending school or studying in another country and staying with a host family. These are not professional businesses and are purely intended to create a true local experience for those wanting to stay in a home setting and live with a local family. Often, local families offer up their homes to schools in the area to be a host family and the homestay guest deals directly with the host family.

Bed and Breakfasts (B&Bs)

B&Bs have been around since travel first began. However, the term itself was coined around World War II in the United Kingdom when foreigners needed a place to stay and people offered rooms in their houses and served breakfast to their guests.[1] B&Bs are usually homes with extra rooms rented to guests (sometimes with private bathrooms) and include breakfast served in the bedroom, a common dining room or kitchen. Unlike homestays, B&Bs are generally run as businesses and the primary intent is to host guests in the home. B&Bs advertise and generally have websites where guests can book direct stays.

Hotels

Since their inception, hotels have always had a direct booking relationship with guests. However, in the last twenty years, the rise of online travel agencies (OTAs) has caused a large proportion of bookings to shift from direct bookings to OTA bookings. This has reduced profitability for hotels, and the pendulum is now starting to swing back, with hotels striving to increase their direct bookings by offering guests lower rates, better terms and exclusive perks that aren't available unless booking directly.

Before platforms existed, guests would find accommodation providers such as homestays, B&Bs and hotels through advertisements, referrals and word of mouth, as well as direct booking websites. Guests booked stays directly with these accommodation providers, and it's only within the last ten years that we've seen an increase in stays being booked through online platforms rather than direct. While these platforms have helped with trust, discoverability and bookings, these advantages have also come at the cost of high fees, resulting in increased prices for guests and lower profitability for businesses. It's also removed the personal touch from the process, turning a personal experience into a commodified travel offering.

The Rise of Direct Bookings

Up until recently, many hosts relied on a single platform for the majority of their revenue. When the COVID-19 pandemic hit and travel ground to a halt, hosts dependent on third-party booking platforms woke up to find their bookings cancelled and their livelihood in jeopardy. Regardless of the booking terms or cancellation policies, guests were refunded, and some platforms even kept their fees, leaving hosts unable to pay for their expenses with no end in sight to the pandemic.

A global pandemic, coupled with travel restrictions, saw swift action by third-party booking platforms, but at the complete disregard for those who contributed the value to these platforms. This caused hosts around the globe to realise that, at the end of the day, as long as they relied on platforms to facilitate bookings, they were at the mercy of these and didn't truly own their business. As Mark Simpson says, "If you rely entirely on platforms, then you have a job, not a business."

As an answer to hosts' outcries against the cancellations, Airbnb introduced a host relief fund. However, the amount of money that individual hosts received was in no way comparable to what they'd lost. In some cases, some hosts received what they called "insulting" amounts, such as Thierry Rignol, who lost over $30,000 because of the cancellations and received $106.02 in "relief" from the fund.[2] Adding insult to injury, less than eight months later, Airbnb went public on the stock market in early December, surging past the $100 billion market cap, making it the biggest initial public offering (IPO) of 2020. While they did offer some hosts the ability to purchase pre-IPO, they limited this to US hosts only,[3] leaving out hosts from the rest of the world who had contributed just as much as hosts in the US to Airbnb's success today.

This created the perfect storm for hosts to realise that they needed a change. In 2019, direct bookings globally made up just 9.24% of bookings compared to other OTA channels, such as Airbnb, Expedia, Vrbo and Booking.com. By 2021, that number jumped to 21.75%, more than doubling in just two years.[4] There's an increasing rise in the global direct booking movement, accelerated by hosts who have had enough of high OTA fees, punitive policies and no ownership in what they're building.

Interestingly, we're seeing evidence that this global trend isn't driven by hosts alone. Guests are waking up to the benefits they receive when booking directly with hosts, such as better service and perks, better rates, lower fees and a more personalised experience without an intermediary. Whether or not you buy into the vision of more ownership and control, the next generation of travellers will be the ultimate drivers of the book direct movement.

For most travellers, the frustration of seeing a significant increase in their nightly rate at checkout due to exorbitant fees that add no additional value to their stay is enough to find creative ways to contact the host directly. This group of travellers are familiar with the direct-to-consumer business model and are tech savvy enough to understand that by circumventing the bureaucratic systems of publicly traded companies and going direct-to-host, they can pay less, receive a better guest experience and have funds left over to actually enjoy their trip. Finally, a growing proportion of these guests understand that there are more efficient and cost-effective ways to transact online.

Since the inception of cryptocurrency, a growing percentage of adopters are pushing to use a new form of money, one that favours self-custody, moves across international borders at the speed of light without need for foreign exchange or credit card processing fees. This once nascent demographic is now taking the world by storm and is moving us from a web2 world in which we have little ownership and control, and into web3.

A Brief Overview of the Web

Web 1.0 (1990–2000)

Although the internet was first created in 1965 and used for military purposes, it wasn't until the late 1980s and early 1990s that it became more widely adopted and used, as internet protocols and technology were standardised and regular people could connect to and use the internet.

The term Web 1.0 was coined in 1989 by Tim Berners-Lee[5] to refer to the first version of the internet, which was called the "read-only" internet – a static version of web pages that allowed users to read material on the internet without the ability to interact with it in any way. They also couldn't provide any feedback, since the structure was only set up for one-way communication from the publishers/developers to consumers without consumers being able to return any information.

To provide a real example, here's Vrbo's website in 1998. It essentially functioned as an online directory that showed properties by state that users could browse through. The listing page provided details about each property, but to book, you had to contact the owner directly via phone or email instead of booking online. For owners who wanted to list or update their listing information, they'd have to contact Vrbo for them to update and publish the changes, as there was no interface for hosts to do this themselves.

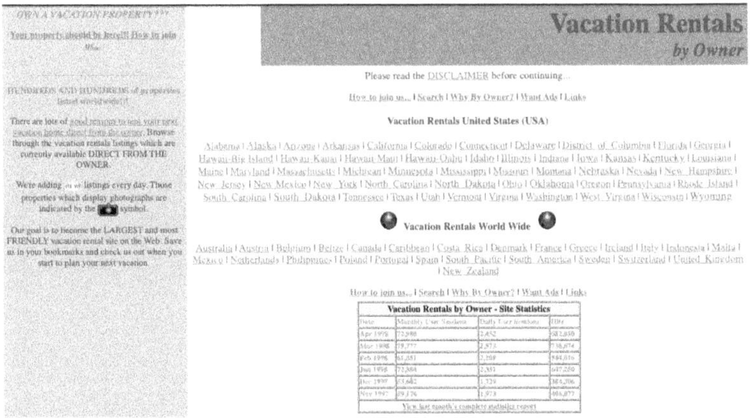
OWN A VACATION PROPERTY???
Your property should be here!!! How to join us...
HUNDREDS AND HUNDREDS of properties listed worldwide!!!
There are lots of good reasons to rent your next vacation home direct from the owner. Browse through the vacation rentals listings which are currently available DIRECT FROM THE OWNER.
We're adding new listings every day. Those properties which display photographs are indicated by the symbol.
Our goal is to become the LARGEST and most FRIENDLY vacation rental site on the Web. Save us in your bookmarks and check us out when you start to plan your next vacation.
Vacation Rentals
by Owner
Please read the DISCLAIMER before continuing...
How to join us... | Search | Why By Owner? | Want Ads | Links
Vacation Rentals United States (USA)
Alabama | Alaska | Arizona | Arkansas | California | Colorado | Connecticut | Delaware | District of Columbia | Florida | Georgia | Hawaii-Big Island | Hawaii-Kauai | Hawaii-Maui | Hawaii-Oahu | Idaho | Illinois | Indiana | Iowa | Kansas | Kentucky | Louisiana | Maine | Maryland | Massachusetts | Michigan | Minnesota | Mississippi | Missouri | Montana | Nebraska | Nevada | New Hampshire | New Jersey | New Mexico | New York | North Carolina | North Dakota | Ohio | Oklahoma | Oregon | Pennsylvania | Rhode Island | South Carolina | South Dakota | Tennessee | Texas | Utah | Vermont | Virginia | Washington | West Virginia | Wisconsin | Wyoming
Vacation Rentals World Wide
Australia | Austria | Belgium | Belize | Canada | Caribbean | Costa Rica | Denmark | France | Greece | Ireland | Italy | Indonesia | Malta | Mexico | Netherlands | Philippines | Poland | Portugal | Spain | South Pacific | South America | Sweden | Switzerland | United Kingdom | New Zealand
How to join us... | Search | Why By Owner? | Want Ads | Links
Vacation Rentals by Owner - Site Statistics
View last month's complete statistics report

New Luxury Condo Directly on the Gulf
Dates available: Year Round
For additional information, contact the owner(s)
Tell them "I saw your ad in Vacation Rentals by Owner"

6, 7

Web 2.0 (2000–Present)

Dale Dougherty defined the term Web 2.0 in 2004 as the "read-write web".[8] This era is called the "read-write" or "write" internet because users have the ability to not only interact with the content from publishers and developers (as well as other people around the world), but to provide feedback on that content. Additionally, and more powerfully, they could create their own content, enabled by platform networks such as Facebook, YouTube, Instagram and other content creation platforms.

As the internet progressed to Web 2.0, the experience became vastly different and progressively interactive. It gave rise to the "platform economy", connecting two sides of a marketplace – supply and demand – in ways that weren't possible previously, spawning entirely new industries and ancillary businesses that service these industries. And it's been a profound global transformation. A total of 5.03 billion people around the world use the internet today – equivalent to 63.1% of the world's population.[9] Airbnb is a primary example of a platform that grew out of Web 2.0 and disrupted the way that people travel around the world by making it mainstream to stay in other people's homes rather than in traditional hotels.

But for all its benefits, Web 2.0 has also caused a behavioural shift in human interaction where users must give away their privacy and data to giant corporations to participate. Aggregated user data and preferences along with intellectual property is Web2's most valuable asset, and consequently corporations are incentivised to close off their ecosystems and lock users into their networks. The creative user content and digital assets belong to the platform rather than users and aren't transferable or valuable outside the scope of the platform.

Readers likely have experienced this firsthand. When you began your journey into short-term rentals, you likely started out on a Web2 platform such as Airbnb, Vrbo, or Booking.com. As you grew your business, you earned a reputation and status within your respective platform, and that status came with various benefits but also tradeoffs. For example, Airbnb Superhosts cannot take their reputation to another platform, and in fact the platform threatens to take away the status if certain rules and behaviours aren't followed. While hosts can technically leave a platform, the loss of a host's reputation that's been painstakingly built up over tens or hundreds of bookings is a significant deterrent to hosts actually being able to leave platforms and provides a thin veil of choice since hosts end up locked into platforms because of assets that are non-transferable.

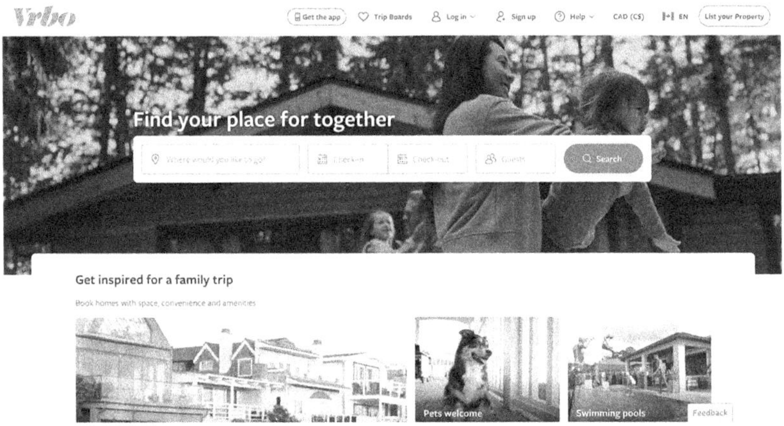

In the Web 1.0 example earlier, Vrbo was a static website that neither hosts nor guests could do much with except read. As the internet progressed to Web 2.0, the experience has become vastly different and progressively interactive. Now, guests can search using an intelligent search engine and also book a property at the same time. Hosts can update their properties in real time and even add their properties to a platform without contacting the website first, unlike in Web 1.0.

Web 3.0 and Web3 (Emerging Now)

Web 3.0 was initially referred to as the "semantic web", termed by Tim Berners-Lee in a 2001 paper.[10] However, the modern Web3 movement (sometimes referred to as the "decentralised web") has a broader meaning. If the pre-internet/web1 era favoured publishers, and the web2 era favoured platforms, the next generation of innovations –

collectively known as web3 – is about tilting the scales of power and ownership back toward creators and users. In the simplest terms, **web3 is an internet owned by users rather than centralised entities.**

The forthcoming wave of web3 goes far beyond the initial use case of cryptocurrencies.

Multiple technologies are emerging to achieve this outcome:

- Blockchain technology to give users control over their data and to democratise access and distribute value and ownership more fairly and equitably across all participants, rather than just the platforms and centralised entities.
- Cryptocurrency tokens distribute the value and is one of the defining principles and mechanisms of the web3 movement.

However, both Web 3.0 and web3 aim to create a better internet and to be an antidote and solution to the largest problems that have arisen from Web 2.0 – primarily the monopoly of centralised entities that collect, store and monetise user data.

It's clear to see that web3 is here to stay. The genie is out of the bottle and companies are realising that if they don't adapt, they will be left behind. It's no surprise that post-pandemic and wary of being able to weather yet another disruption, the travel industry is looking to lead the web3 revolution. Major airlines are experimenting with NFT (Non-Fungible Token) ticketing and offering cryptocurrency payment options. Hotels are adopting blockchain-based inventory management systems to eliminate data fragmentation errors. Even though web3 will most certainly alter travel as we know it today, the groundbreaking technology will, for the first time in history, shift the balance of power from large, centralised organisations, and into the hands of the individual and small-to-medium sized businesses.

Progressive Web3 Blueprint: Direct stays powered by people like you within a connected hospitality ecosystem

Though there are many segments within travel, few stand to benefit more than the short-term and vacation rental industry. With some of the most intelligent engineers and developers moving into web3, the foundational framework now exists for hosts to operate a direct booking business yet benefit from demand driven by a network of travellers who prefer to book direct. Though web3 is new technology, the problems it's solving are real problems being faced today.

This was backed up by the research Dtravel conducted with hundreds of hosts to learn what their biggest challenges and desires were. The recurrent theme was ownership: hosts want increased ownership over their funds, policies, terms and conditions, decisions that affect them, and ownership in the businesses they're helping to build by contributing to them. We were excited to learn this because ownership is key to the ethos of the web3 movement. It's about taking ownership from the hands of a few monopolies and distributing that ownership and value to everyone who contributes.

These problems exist because existing structures and incentives create a zero-sum game – in order for one side to win, the other side must lose. For example, if Airbnb makes a decision to the benefit of guests, the host loses. If the platform benefits, both hosts and guests lose. Platforms have to be extractive as they grow in order to become profitable and give investors and shareholders returns.

In the same way, there are problems guests experience because of web2 structures. Fees have become exorbitant, often resulting in prices that exceed those of hotels, an industry that platforms set out to disrupt. Stays have become transactional without a personal touch because platforms have interjected themselves in the middle, creating distance between hosts and guests. Platforms lack loyalty and rewards programmes, providing zero benefit for staying loyal to them. Guests also lack ownership in the businesses they use, despite being the ones to drive revenue and encourage others to spend their money by travelling with them.

Using web3 technologies such as smart contracts and cryptocurrencies enable these web2 problems to be solved in a fundamentally different way, without the shortcomings and structural failures inherent in web2. In order to break out of unfair structures, you have to create new paradigms that aim to solve problems differently and this is the place that web3 occupies.

Direct bookings are growing as a movement and web3 will accelerate this trend through a technology layer designed to empower hosts. Web3 is here to stay, and the future is a connected hospitality ecosystem that benefits those who contribute value.

Hosting is a close-knit community, yet closed systems and gated platforms prevent access and permission to build. Imagine an ecosystem where hosts come together and decide they want to build a host supply marketplace, the community votes on the proposal, and develops the initiative through a community treasury funded by fees earned through the ecosystem. Hosts benefit and the operators of the host marketplace benefit because they're encouraged to be part of the ecosystem. This is completely counter to how ancillary services and companies work today – they're kept at the sidelines instead of being brought into the ecosystem where everyone can benefit. The more valuable contributors that become part of the ecosystem, the more it grows and the more value it has, which benefits everyone who is an owner in the ecosystem. This is the difference between web2 platforms today and healthy and thriving web3 ecosystems that are being built for tomorrow.

The Blueprint for Your Web3 Hospitality Business

If you're ready to begin your journey towards digital ownership and self-sovereignty and want the blueprint to start your web3 hospitality business, here are a few fundamentals to get started.

Independent Property Management Systems (PMS) / Channel Managers (CM)

A PMS is software that assists short-term rental hosts and vacation rental property managers in managing their listings, bookings, payments and/or communication with guests. By having the ability to organise operations across several properties and platforms in a single place, hosts can access convenient tools to efficiently take care of administrative tasks, saving both time and operational expenses.

When selecting a PMS, choose one that allows you to be the Merchant of Record (MOR). This is critical to truly owning your hospitality business because being the MOR allows you to keep the flow of funds in your own hands, versus the funds flowing through someone else's account, such as a platform. Also important is finding a PMS or CM that values and empowers your independence as a brand and business and has the tools to help you own more aspects of your business. Finally, choose one that iterates and changes according to market and technological shifts, so that you can do the same.

Web3 Technology

Cryptocurrency Payments

As we alluded to earlier, the younger generation of travellers – Millennials and Gen Z – are engaging in new and different ways with different expectations. They want cryptocurrency payment options that are borderless, without exchange fees or banks, low or no fees and self-custody over their funds.

Millennials have overtaken Baby Boomers as the largest adult cohort around the world with 1.8 billion millennials, equal to 23% of the global population.[11] Gen Z makes up the largest overall cohort in the world, making up 26% of the global population with over 2 billion Gen Z-ers.[12] Together, they make up 49% of the global population and businesses that ignore the needs of these two generations do so at their peril. It's estimated that 1 billion people will use cryptocurrencies in 2022.[13]

People are already using cryptocurrency to book travel. Travala, a leading cryptocurrency OTA, sees 80% of its bookings in cryptocurrencies[14] and monthly booking revenue averaging $5 million or more.[15] Incorporating cryptocurrency payment options isn't a "nice to have" but a "must have" in this quickly changing global economy for hospitality entrepreneurs, especially as Millennials and Gen Z age up and overtake Baby Boomers in spending.

The good news is that there are easy ways to incorporate crypto payments as infrastructure has come very far in the last few years. There are multiple crypto payment options that hosts can incorporate into their websites to accept crypto easily.

Non-fungible tokens (NFTs)

Non-fungible tokens (NFTs) are cryptocurrency tokens that represent a unique asset, where ownership can be cryptographically proven. NFTs have exploded in mainstream awareness and popularity, with large brands such as Nike, Gucci, Pepsi, Adidas and the NBA issuing their own NFTs. In the travel space, airlines such as Air Baltic and Emirates and hotel brands such as Marriott are using NFTs to increase loyalty and engagement and build awareness among the younger demographic.

It's an inevitability that NFTs and tokens will replace outdated, opaque and ineffective loyalty programmes. It will soon become the norm, in the same way that loyalty points today are. NFTs can also be used to represent a room night, which can then be purchased and sold by anyone on a marketplace, which the accommodation provider can charge a secondary sale royalty for, adding a new revenue stream. This provides more flexibility for travellers and reduces cancellations for accommodation providers.

Issuing NFTs for special campaigns or repeat guests is fairly simple with many NFT issuing platforms on the market, many of which don't require technical skills to use.

The world of NFTs is vast and still nascent and there's a lot of exciting innovation still to be explored and built. Learning ahead of the curve will give businesses a significant advantage when this technology becomes as ubiquitous as loyalty programmes.

Hospitality Communities

With the rise and popularity of STR/VR OTAs, the hosting community has banded together and formed tight-knit communities that help each other, share hosting tips and even refer guests to each other. There are many types of communities based on location or geography, type of host (e.g. VR, STR, pro or casual) and even global communities. Facebook groups are a good place to find hosts such as yourself, whether by geography or another interest. Get involved in a group, meet other hosts and perhaps even consider joining other hospitality associations so you have more ways to drive bookings to your business and become less reliant on platforms.

The future of short-term and vacation rentals will ultimately be free from the misaligned incentives of third-party platforms, offering a fair distribution of control and economic benefit to those who contribute value. Hosts and property managers will operate without intermediaries yet have a democratic voice in the future direction of the technological infrastructure and ecosystem that enables secure, transparent and cost-efficient direct bookings. The future of short-term and vacation rentals is with Dtravel.

What is Dtravel?

Our vision is to enable community members, including hosts and guests, to work together to build and realise the full potential of a new travel experience. We want to create a world where every person is empowered to be a member in the future success of the ownership economy. At the heart of everything we do, it's about ownership and empowering everyone within our ecosystem to become owners.

The reason we focus on ownership is because this is what we heard from hosts over and over again worldwide in the interviews we conducted with them. Hosts want more control over their policies and funds, and ownership in the products they've helped build into billion-dollar publicly traded businesses.

Based on this research, we created Dtravel's direct booking product. We're providing hosts with infrastructure that enables them to accept on-chain bookings via a new web3 ecosystem that blends the freedom of direct booking sites with the simplicity of OTAs, offering unrivalled ownership and control over the entire booking process.

The core idea behind Dtravel is to enable hosts and guests to transact with each other in a peer-to-peer manner without any intermediaries. Dtravel is not a platform but instead functions as a technology provider that creates easy-to-use web3 tools for travel participants to use, which drastically reduces fees, improves host-guest relationships and creates a fairer, autonomous and transparent booking ecosystem in the process. We make it incredibly easy to realise the benefits of web3 without the need to have any technical knowledge or experience in the field.

What makes Dtravel unique and different, and where the web3 benefits come in, is in: (1) smart contract technology; and (2) Dtravel's native token TRVL.

Smart Contract Technology

We use smart contracts to power the booking engine, which are software programmes built on blockchains that automatically execute based on predetermined rules without the need for intervention.

To create a property listing on Dtravel, property managers and hosts set the booking conditions – such as the price per night, cleaning fee and cancellation policy – just as they would on vacation and short-term rental platforms. These conditions are added to a smart contract unique to each listing, and when a guest makes a booking, the details of that booking are cryptographically signed and included in the on-chain booking transaction, along with the booking payment. The transaction is then sent to the listing's smart contract to be held in a decentralised escrow account. Once the cancellation period ends, the smart contract will automatically release the funds to the host, provided the guest doesn't cancel within this period. This is all automatically done via smart contract technology, and no one can change the terms of the booking or override policies once a booking is underway.

Most importantly, for any hosts using this smart contract technology, Dtravel has created the infrastructure so that these smart contracts are owned by the host. This is crucial because it allows hosts to use this smart contract-powered booking engine without relying on a third party, such as a platform or payment processor. No matter what, hosts can accept payments uninterrupted. We've seen countless times where a platform removes a host or a payment processor closes an account – sometimes without warning, notice or reason – and completely shuts down the host's business, since they have no way to accept payments. With Dtravel's smart contract-powered booking engine, hosts no longer need to rely on any intermediary to continue accepting payments.

Because the smart contracts are automated via software programs without the need for manual intervention, this drastically reduces fees, which are passed on to both hosts and guests on Dtravel. Another benefit of the smart contract technology is that it enables cryptocurrencies as payment options, reducing transaction fees from services such as Stripe (which charges roughly 3%) down to effectively 0% for payment fees.

Dtravel uses stablecoins – cryptocurrencies that are pegged to and backed by government-issued US dollars – as payment options to significantly reduce the volatility of the funds that hosts receive from bookings.

Dtravel's Native Token TRVL

Dtravel is owned by its members who hold the TRVL token. You can think of this like an online collective that is co-owned by its members who vote on decisions.

As a token holder, you can vote on proposals and decisions that affect everyone in the ecosystem. This was another piece of feedback we heard from hosts – they wanted to have input on decisions that would directly affect them. This model helps to meet this need by giving everyone the opportunity to vote on key decisions. Holding the TRVL token also gives members ownership of the ecosystem. Hosts, guests and community members who contribute to the Dtravel ecosystem will receive TRVL as rewards for adding value and helping to grow the ecosystem, making them co-owners and co-creators in the ecosystem.

As we mentioned earlier, empowering hosts to truly own their businesses is at the core of what we believe in. This is why we're building technology that gives hosts the power to run their businesses as they desire without the risk that a third party can shut it down at any time. We saw firsthand throughout the pandemic how much hosts were affected by these platforms overriding their policies and putting their businesses at risk or even completely out of business, and this is something we never want to see happen again.

The Best of Both Worlds

The overreliance on third-party booking platforms has come about because these platforms made it easy for hosts to list their properties. But the tradeoff has resulted in a loss of control and a commoditisation of the host and guest relationship because of intermediaries. When building a solution to address hosts' concerns around control and ownership, we knew that it was crucial for us to create an experience that was just as easy as using an OTA without losing the benefits of ownership that are so important to hosts.

Dtravel gives hosts the ownership and control of a direct booking website with the ease of using an OTA. As a direct booking site powered by web3 technologies, it's just as easy to use as web2 platforms, though with complete control over your policies and funds in a way that isn't possible with web2 solutions. You can think of us as a Shopify for the vacation and short-term rental industry, powering bookings without centralisation or reliance on third-party payment processors. Just as Shopify powers ecommerce stores on the backend, Dtravel powers bookings on the backend, with one major difference: hosts are truly the owners of their businesses.

We know this is just the beginning, and helping hosts with search and discoverability will be important in helping them grow their businesses. Dtravel's metasearch experience for guests will drive demand and help with listing discovery, all without the need for an intermediary. The metasearch function will pull in results for all direct booking sites (think Skyscanner) with the ability for guests to search for Dtravel-powered listings specifically. The intention is to empower all hosts with direct booking sites – not just Dtravel direct booking listings – to be able to grow their businesses, because we believe that direct bookings are what is best for the industry in the long run.

The Direct Booking Movement is a Web3 Movement

The direct booking movement has exploded and is growing quickly because of the benefits and values driving it: more control, direct relationships with guests, lower fees and ownership over your brand and reputation. Web3 has the same values: ownership over your funds, lower fees and ownership in your identity, reputation and ultimately the value that you help to create.

This is why we believe that the direct booking movement is a web3 movement. Web3 serves to accelerate and strengthen all the benefits of direct bookings, and hosts get all the same benefits of a direct booking website but with the added benefits of true ownership over funds and payment processing and ownership in the ecosystem.

We are at the cusp of the next era of the internet, where corporations are no longer the ones in control, where there's a fairer and more equitable distribution of value and where every person is empowered to be an active owner and contributor in the ecosystems that they participate in. We believe in web3 to create a better world, and we want to be the catalyst for this change in the travel industry.

We want to help hosts who believe that there's a better way to host, one where they form direct relationships with their guests, where they own their own businesses without someone else overriding their policies and where they get ownership in the value they help to create. If you're ready for a new travel ecosystem, one where there are no users but only owners, we welcome you to become an owner with us.

To claim your free Boostly NFT and learn more about Dtravel head to **bookdirectblueprint.com**

HOW TO OFFER UPSELLS TO YOUR GUESTS

MADI RIFKIN – MOUNT

Mount started from an idea I had when I was twelve: to build a lock onto my bike. I did this out of pure necessity, as I was the forgetful child who couldn't remember my lock for the life of me. Little did I know that inventing my lock would propel me on an epic journey of entrepreneurship. I grew up an entrepreneur; I sold candy, custom stickers and worked any other side hustle to help me earn money. Following that path, I acquired a patent at fifteen for the lock I had developed when I was twelve. From then, my life goal was to become a billionaire, and in my mind the only way to get there was to start my own company.

Mount's founding journey and problem discovery happened during a very turbulent time in our world: the middle of the COVID-19 pandemic, one of the largest disrupting events in the recent history of the travel industry. The way people travel had changed forever. Travellers turned to local one-hour drive destinations to avoid flying. They turned away from hotel rooms and towards STRs. They were taking longer trips while working remotely. Mount needed a way to capitalise on this shift in travel, so we leaned into it. As people look for more than just a place to stay, Mount is optimising our product offering and brand to capture the new traveller, led by Gen Zs who demand exciting experiences at every destination. We want to educate the Gen-Zs to rent instead of buy, travel with a backpack, and have an enjoyable, memorable adventure. How can Mount help all those involved in the travel industry, STR space and beyond to cater to this new traveller as the world has officially evolved?

Mount as it stands today does not involve bike locks, but it involves my other lifelong passion: travel. I grew up travelling. I spent my summer vacations abroad hopping from country to country where I learned ancient Greek history, WWII history, and most importantly, everything that went into planning and organising trips. My core memories from when I was six are of myself and my family of sixteen travelling the world. I have even been to more countries than I have US states.

All of these trips had something in common: being a family, and adventuring together. Many of the changes that morphed Mount from a bike lock company to one redefining the travel experience are directly attributable to my experiences during my journeys. Mount became a way to connect locals to tourists through rentable amenities and experiences.

The first memory that comes to mind is a backpacking trip through Europe with my best friend, and now investor, Cindy. We were hopping from STR to STR, and having never backpacked before, we took the term quite literally. I stuffed all my clothes into a Patagonia backpack; Cindy took the duffle bag route. Needless to say, we were travelling while lugging around 30+ pound bags from country to country. We started in Sweden, then hopped to Norway, where we made a pit stop to meet my distant Norwegian cousins. Eventually, we found ourselves in Amsterdam. Throughout all this time travelling, I couldn't help but feel like we stood out, and not in a good way. I got the feeling we were being categorised as "dumb American" tourists. I couldn't find the right clothes, I didn't speak the right language, and everywhere we went we ended up in some kind of tourist trap, when all I really wanted was to explore like a local. It wasn't until we got to our Airbnb at our last stop in Amsterdam that I finally felt like I could fit in. The reason? Our host had left two bikes for us to use during our stay.

Now, if you are familiar with Amsterdam, you know that everyone there gets around on bikes, so I was eager to jump in on the action. At first, we were slightly hesitant. We did not know the area. However, we eventually got on the bikes, and I was so glad we did. I immediately started to blend in and the feeling of being a tourist slowly subsided. I felt like a local. I wanted to take this feeling with me everywhere I travelled. Why couldn't all Airbnb hosts supply or even offer these amazing amenities at an extra cost, like the bikes we were given in Amsterdam? I was left with this thought as I travelled back to the States to start my third year at Northeastern University, where I was studying entrepreneurship.

At this time, I had been working on Mount Locks, a lock company for the emerging micromobility market – think of those crazy scooters that are left everywhere in cities. I mulled over my Amsterdam experience until I had another rather strange travel experience.

Fast forward two years; I'm a graduate of Northeastern University and I have just moved to Hawaii to fully pursue Mount full-time. My co-founder Rishab and I had been accepted into a startup accelerator called Blue Startups, and Mount had just made its pivot into the short-term rental space. I had taken a few scooters from the micromobility industry and placed them at some Airbnb properties. I wasn't sure what we had stumbled upon, but I knew two things: tourists loved scooters and young people travelled to Airbnbs. What we soon discovered was that these scooters became a new revenue stream for the host. Tourists were renting the scooters using our software and hosts were collecting the extra rental revenue. We operated that way for a few months.

I had my, "WOW I really need Mount right now!" moment when my co-founder Rishab and I were travelling and living in Hawaii for three months. We'd gone down to Hawaii to participate in Blue Startups, where we dove deep into Mount and grew the business. Naturally, since we were in Hawaii, we liked to go to the beach and hike on the weekends, but because we were only going to be there for three months, we didn't bring much with us other than clothing. One weekend, we decided to go to a beach on the North Shore of Oahu. I'd got used to sitting on the sand with my towel while really wishing I could just go right up to the house on the beach and use Mount to rent a beach chair, cooler and umbrella for the day.

While relaxing on the beach, Rishab decided it would be a great time to go and try to find a kayak to rent. In Hawaii, renting amenities directly on the beach isn't allowed, so he had to walk twenty minutes back to our car and drive a mile to a kayak rental shop that he had found on Google. I didn't know any of this until he returned four hours later. Finally, I got a text saying he was on his way back, and that he would pick me up. I gathered my things and walked up to the road where I waited for him to arrive. A few minutes passed before I saw this car appear from around the bend. It looked like our car, but there was a massive kayak strapped to the roof. I use the term "strapped to" VERY loosely. The kayak was sitting precariously on our roof, with one strap tying it down. To my dismay, the kayak shop hadn't mentioned that they were closing for the day, and Rishab hadn't returned his kayak in time. Therefore, he was stuck with a 24-hour rental while I, unknowingly, got locked into an hour-plus drive around the island with a teetering kayak strapped to our roof that could fall off at any moment. There are so many things that went wrong that could have been avoided if the short-term rentals were using Mount. Rishab could have got his kayak rental from one of the STRs near the beach. All rentals with Mount are self-service, so the "virtual" rental shop never closes. He could return the kayak whenever he was done with it, no matter if it was 6pm or 1am.

Ask yourself: have you ever had an experience where Mount would have made a world of difference? Could it have made your life easier and more enjoyable?

After this experience and a few more just like it, I realised the necessity of Mount from a host's perspective in wanting new revenue streams, but also from the traveller's perspective. They are seeking out easy, enjoyable and convenient experiences.

Now, I tell you this story for a few reasons.

Why Travellers Want Upsells

Based on our first-hand kayak rental experience in Hawaii, as travellers, we found some downsides to the traditional amenity rental process:

1. The process of finding a place to rent amenities is inconvenient and cumbersome, on top of the fact the shop is a mile away from the beach. Why was this so inconvenient?
2. This was not a self-service rental, so people had to be present to rent and return the equipment. Why wasn't this solved with technology?
3. Our beach was surrounded by rental properties loaded with

fun beach toys and equipment. Why can't travellers see what's available to rent and grab it for a few hours?

These questions, coupled with my Amsterdam experience, prompted me to investigate why there wasn't a marketplace that connected travellers to local amenity rentals.

Why it is Hard to Offer Upsells to Your Guests

After conducting extensive research to determine why Airbnb hosts/ property managers were not offering these types of amenities, I narrowed it down to three main factors:

1. There is no payment processing tool for offering these types of amenities. If you want to offer your guests bikes, you need to do so for free or somehow chase them down and collect cash. There's no automation for this.

2. There is no cost-effective insurance policy to rent amenities like bikes, scooters, or golf carts to your guests without taking on an enormous amount of liability. A typical rental policy costs anywhere from $10,000-$100,000 a year.

3. There is no management tool to provide transparency in offering these amenities. You don't know how the guest is going to use them. If your amenities are damaged and if they get lost or stolen, how do you find them?

During my research, I came across a few hosts/property managers who had figured out the key to offering upsells and had optimised it for their own properties. One of those hosts was Kevin, who I met via the app Clubhouse. He owns and operates a single eight-bedroom house on the coast of Canada. He had optimised his property to the point that he brought in just as much revenue from upsell experiences as he did from his booking revenue. That one property pulls in over $1M a year in upsell revenue. He curates his guests' entire stay and chooses a theme, whether it be a family-fun vacation that includes a boat day trip, private chef dinners, or a bachelorette girls' trip that includes a yacht party and private pizza party. Now, this is doable because Kevin has one property and has optimised it for upsell experiences. He went out, curated all the necessary relationships and brokered revenue splits with all the experiences he directly books. This is possible because Kevin handles all the bookings for the experiences and his guests don't have to lift a finger. Where things get a little tricky is when a host has more than one property and is trying to do this for multiple guests in multiple locations. It is nearly impossible to track revenue/affiliate shares when everything is done by a word-of-mouth agreement, especially at scale! This is exactly why Mount exists – we enable hosts, property managers and hoteliers to offer these amazing rentable amenities by solving those three core issues. Mount is a software platform that takes your electric bike and makes it rentable and trackable, all while fully insuring it and relieving you and your property from liability. Mount makes it possible to create and automate new revenue streams at your property, so that you don't increase your workload, but double your revenue.

This was a key discovery. Property managers, hosts, hotels – they all had the same problem: how do I make more money at my property without creating extra work? This insight allowed Mount to go from a scooter renting platform to a software platform that can open new revenue streams at short-term rentals. We do this by turning assets into rentable amenities and automating the entire process, including payments, insurance, management and even the offerings themselves. We either take the assets you already own, or help find you new ones at a discount, or supply them to you for free through our "Co-host" programme. Our Co-host programme is a bit of a selective process; you must apply, but if chosen, you have the opportunity to receive free e-bikes, beach chairs, kayaks, paddle boards – you name it! To top it all off, we provide a co-host who will run the program for you. They will perform any necessary maintenance and locate any lost assets if that happens.

Why it is Important to Offer Upsells

Travellers are looking at their accommodation as part of their experience, so it needs to live up to their expectations. What does this mean for hosts, property managers and hotels? *They need to start offering more experiences*. Currently, 83% of all travellers are seeking out and willingly paying for these experiences. Globally, travellers are spending around $9.3 billion dollars for these activities.

If you are a host, property manager, or hotel, are you offering your guests experiences? If so, you should not be offering these for free: you should consider these "experience upsells". Let me explain what I mean by experience upsell. It could be as simple as placing four electric bikes at your property for rent and suggesting to your guests that they rent the bikes and go to local brewery X or local restaurant Y. Electric bikes have the opportunity to rent from $60-$120 a day depending on the location and season. How often does a guest ask their host for local recommendations, or a boat ride recommendation, or a rental shop to rent something? This is all revenue the host should be capitalising on one way or another. That is exactly why Mount exists.

Mount creates and automates new revenue streams for properties while avoiding adding extra work to your day. Below are a few examples of how we have worked with hosts to open up new revenue streams to replicate Kevin's model where property owners could be making at least 50% more on top of their other revenue streams.

One of Mount's hosts, Taylor, owner and operator of an STR property in Upstate New York, is building an automated upsell house that can be replicated and scaled. Taylor uses Mount to rent firewood bundles and s'mores kits to her guests, in addition to offering electric bike rentals. She wants to offer upsells and an incredible guest experience but doesn't want to waste time curating and customising every guest trip. She uses Mount for that unique experience feel and to increase her revenue, but she doesn't feel any impact to her workload. Once property owners incorporate Mount into their guest experiences, it does the work for them – all they have to do is remind their guests that there are amenities for rent at the property.

Another host found us out of necessity. Brooke is the owner and operator of a four-bedroom beach house in Miramar Beach, Florida. Her property is within the Destin Golf and Beach Resort, which allows guests access to a private beach. She was offering a golf cart and beach equipment to her guests, but the rub is that she lives full-time in another state. She visits the property for a few weeks out of the year when she and her family are using it to vacation. Otherwise, she relies on the cleaners to inform her of any damage. Prior to using Mount, Brooke had a beach closet with chairs, umbrellas and boogie boards that she allowed her guests to use. She relied on the honour system and expected guests to bring back the gear after each use. She didn't know if the guests were using it, couldn't charge extra for the usage, and ended up losing some of the equipment because there was no way to track it. Mount came in and turned that equipment into a beach bundle comprised of four folding Tommy Bahama chairs, a cooler, wagon, and an umbrella that can be rented out to guests. Mount connected the bundle to our app, so now when a guest wants to use the beach equipment, they go through our rental process, and are accountable for returning the equipment. Since implementing Mount, Brooke has had no lost items and even no reported damage! The cherry on top – her guests are paying for the rentals anywhere from $30-50 a day. One of her guests left this note:

"We used the beach bundle every time we went to the beach. It was very convenient and easy to use."
– Guest

Another property that came to Mount was the Fairmont Grand Del Mar in San Diego. They had purchased six electric Rad power bikes during the pandemic to offer to their guests. They wanted to rent them to guests but didn't know how, and had no way of collecting payment. They worked with Mount to onboard their six bikes to the Mount platform and made them rentable using our app. Again, instead of adding additional work, Mount streamlined the process. The guests can rent the e-bikes by downloading the Mount app and following the prompts within the app to get started. Mount's geo-fencing technology ensures that the e-bikes are rented from a specific location and brought back to the same location. A guest cannot end a rental until they are back on the hotel property. The hotel also has the ability to track the e-bikes in real-time with Mount's GPS tracking system. The hotel is loving the program and bringing in $700-$1,000 a month.

How to Offer Upsells Using Mount

Mount brings both parties together, so everyone involved has an enjoyable experience. Mount's core offering allows users to travel light.

With just their backpack, travellers can rent everything they need at their destination by using the Mount app. The platform connects travellers to locals who supply add-on amenities like e-bikes, scooters, surfboards, golf clubs, firewood and more!

Mount is a marketplace for the sharing economy that's rooted in travel. We give hosts using Airbnb, Vrbo and other platforms the opportunity to rent almost everything (just not their house!). Not only does Mount stand on its own as a platform, it has the potential to integrate with any of the vacation rental booking giants. Our platform makes authentically unexpected exploration possible while empowering hosts, travellers and locals in ways that open up the shared economy, and lighten up everyone's baggage.

To add amenities to your property, go to **bookdirectblueprint.com** where you can find out how to list your property on Mount in only five minutes.

THE
BOOK DIRECT
BLUEPRINT

Enjoying the book so far?

Leave a review on
Amazon and send proof to
info@boostly.co.uk
for a special (bonus) training!

TAMING RISK

HUMPHREY BOWLES – SUPERHOG

"You cannot escape the responsibility of tomorrow by evading it today."
Abe Lincoln

Intro

One cold, dark winter's night during one of the many German air raids on Moscow during the Second World War, a distinguished Soviet professor of statistics showed up at his local air-raid shelter. He had never appeared there before. "There are seven million people in Moscow," he used to say. "Why should I expect a bomb to hit me?" His friends, who were extremely surprised to see him, asked what had caused him to change his mind. "Look," he explained, "there are seven million people in Moscow and one elephant. Last night they got the elephant."

So, what do short-term rentals, Soviet professors and bombed elephants have in common? Well, I know many property managers who approach every booking like the professor before the elephant was hit. I was one of them. We know the horror stories, we know the statistics, but we bet that nothing will happen to us. We predict what will and what will not happen in the future using nothing but our gut and experience. Experience counts for a lot, but it is poor armour against the sophisticated tools of today's criminal underworld.

We all agree that having complete knowledge of the future is an impossibility, but what leads us to go from hope to proactive prevention? What counts for more, the thousands of successful bookings in the past or the one potential bomb of tomorrow? In this chapter, I'm going to take you on a whistlestop tour of risk, luck, gambling or insurance, and risk management. I hope reading this chapter will make you feel empowered, motivated and invigorated to break free of relying on anyone else but you. I want to help you understand short-term rental risk in a new way, and I want to help you convert blind risk-taking into knowledge and control. Like Prometheus, you will be able to defy the OTA gods, you will succeed in probing the darkness in search of the fire, light and warmth. The fire of direct bookings, the light of avoiding the wrong guests, and the warmth of generating new revenue. In all, I'm going to show you how you can tame risk and unleash opportunity.

Risk

"The biggest risk a person can take is to do nothing."
Robert T. Kiyosaki

The first question every owner asks is how much money can I make? The second, what happens if something goes wrong?

The word "risk" derives from the early Italian *risicare*, which means "to dare". Risk touches on the most profound aspects of psychology and experience. In simple terms, risk is the possibility of something bad happening. In short-term rentals, risk is an ever-present shadow; a broken wine glass, scuff marks on the walls or guests 'filling up' their EV without permission. Or the risk of a damaged bed, stained carpets, or loss of income due to a walkout as the air-conditioning is not working. Of course, there are also the extremes. Risk ultimately draws us to certain OTAs and puts us off others. It's the reason some property managers are happy to give up large percentages of margin and it's also a reason property managers can be fearful of taking direct bookings.

No one can dispute that short-term rentals risk is real; every single day, we face a multitude of malfunctions, errors, parties, shootings, lootings and worse. And all this risk is embraced in the full knowledge that it exists. It's a question of when, not if, the elephant is going to get hit again. This creates fear and fear is hugely destructive. I find it hard to separate fear from risk, as clearly the amount of perceived fear drives the amount of risk someone is willing to take. Fear is one of the most basic human emotions. It is programmed into the nervous system and works like an instinct. From the time we're children, we are equipped with the survival instincts necessary to respond with fear when we sense danger or feel unsafe. A real fear we have, and therefore a risk to overcome, is our epigenetic fear of strangers. Our fear of strangers is one of the most widely shared fears humans have and short-term rentals is all about interacting with strangers. It is more complicated than this, though, just as it was for the professor.

In short-term rentals, as we have discussed, risk has always been there, but it's never been more important than it is today. In the fifties and sixties, having guests to stay was sublimely simple. Brochures akin to the yellow pages would arrive, all sent to "People Like U and Me". Communication was simple, risk nullified and there were very few concerns. This was more the era of home-exchanging than renting, which meant the biggest issue was the delicious Mexican stand-off at the end of the booking around how clean your guests were going to leave your home and how clean you should leave theirs. This doesn't mean that incidents didn't happen, they did, but repairs could be made without calling the plumber, the electrician, or call centres. And, what is more, failure for one property manager seldom had a direct impact on another even if they were based next door.

The fear the professor felt after the untimely end of the elephant demonstrates the internal dilemmas that run through us as human beings. A single event is enough for any of us to change our behaviour and beliefs when it comes to facing risk. This is a huge point to get across. Put another way, a disaster that happens in California can have an impact on the sentiment of other hosts, owners and property managers all over the world. An all-night rave in London could lead to an owner in Charleston removing their property as the risk is now perceived to be too great. Breakdowns can be catastrophic, with far-reaching consequences, not just for the victim, but for the industry. The internet, social media, news, all amplifies fear and risk, and therefore how we understand, consume, and make decisions on it must also be updated.

We can assemble big pieces of information and little pieces, but we can never get all the pieces together. We never know for sure how good our information is. This uncertainty is what makes arriving at judgements so difficult and acting on them so risky. When information is lacking, or we do not have the right tools, we have to fall back on reasoning to try to guess the odds. Guessing leads us to some curious conclusions as we try to cope with the uncertainties we face and the risks we take. Apparently, most people overestimate the information available to them, especially when they are afraid.

The most daring idea that I want to put to you is that vacation rental uncertainty, short-term rental risk, can be tamed. Uncertainty means turning known unknowns into known knowns. It's about understanding what risks we should take and what information is relevant. I am not the prophet of doom, as the capacity to manage risk, and with it the appetite to take risk and make forward-looking choices, are key elements of the energy that drives the short-term rental sector forward. First though, let's address another elephant in the room: luck.

Luck

"Luck always seems to be against the man who depends on it."
Ukrainian Proverb

Just what do we mean by luck?

"Last night they got the elephant." Our favourite explanation for such an event is to ascribe it to luck, good or bad as the case may be. If everything is a matter of luck, risk management is a meaningless exercise. Invoking luck obscures truth because it separates an event from its cause.

When we say that someone has fallen on bad luck, we take away from that person any responsibility for what has happened. When we say that someone has good luck, we deny that person credit for the effort that might have led to the happy outcome. But how sure can we be? Was it fate or choice that decided the outcome?

Until we can distinguish between an event that is truly random and an event that is the result of cause and effect, we will never know whether what we see is what we'll get, nor how we got what we got. When we take a risk, we are betting on an outcome that will result from a decision we have made, though we do not know for certain what the outcome will be.

The essence of risk management lies in maximising the areas where we have some control over the outcome while minimising the areas where we have absolutely no control over the outcome and the linkage between effect and cause is hidden from us.

Every property manager has the ability to influence every single booking. Luck does not need to play a part. The key questions to answer about each and every guest are:

1. Who is the guest?
2. Can you trust them?
3. What happens if something goes wrong?

By being able to answer these questions, luck can be relegated to the background. If we do this effectively, then like casinos and insurers, we can swing the odds into our favour.

~~Insurance~~ Gambling

"There are worse things in life than death. Have you ever spent an evening with an insurance agent?"
Woody Allen

Why is it most of us gamble now and then, compared to why we regularly pay premiums to an insurance company? The mathematical probabilities indicate that we will lose money in both instances. In the case of gambling, it is statistically impossible to expect, though possible to achieve, more than a break-even, because the house tilts the odds against us. In the case of insurance, the premiums we pay exceed the statistical odds that our house will burn down. In both cases, the house always wins; we lose. But why do we enter into these losing propositions? Why do we trust insurers to look after us "when the worst happens" and the casino to pay out when we win the jackpot?

Putting aside that for most people we gamble for entertainment rather than risk, the psychology is that we gamble because we are willing to accept the large possibility of a small loss in the tiny hope of winning a large gain. When we buy insurance, we do so as we cannot afford to take the risk of losing our home to fire, or we are legally obliged to purchase insurance for the protection of others. Put into gambling speak, we accept a gamble that will almost certainly result in a small loss (the premium we pay) but deliver a large gain if catastrophe strikes, compared to a gamble with a certain small gain (not paying a premium) but with uncertain but potentially ruinous consequences for us or our family.

We often face the possibility that we will make the wrong choice and end up regretting it. Short-term rentals are not like a game of roulette at a casino. Averages are useful guides on some occasions but misleading on many others. It never runs black, red, black, red, black. On still other occasions, numbers by themselves, like guests with no reviews, are no help at all and we are obliged to creep into the future guided by only other data points. Numbers are not useless in real life. The trick is to develop a sense of when they are relevant and when they are not. For instance, which defines the risk of being hit by a bomb, seven million people or one elephant?

The premium we pay the insurance company is only one of many certain costs we pay in order to avoid the possibility of a larger, uncertain loss, and we go to great lengths to protect ourselves from the consequences of being wrong. But let me give you some straight whisky regarding property damage insurance and short-term rentals; insurance is a sub-optimal solution. It's a loss you don't need to take or pay for. First, insurance companies can only stay in business if they make more money on premiums than they pay out via claims. The premiums collected from their customers have to cover the claim pay-outs as well as give enough profit to pay the insurer's overheads and pay the agent's overheads plus everyone else in the deal, for example paying claims, marketing and customer services. Put this another way, if you beat the house then it's likely the house will dump you as a client. Secondly, it requires a disaster to be beneficial. Catastrophe striking, losing one's elephant, is not the same as spilt wine or suitcase marks going up the stairs. Thirdly, as a host, one of your goals is to protect your owners' properties. Insurance totally fails at this as it will not stop incidents from happening, it will only pay out after disaster has happened. Anyone who accepts that this is something they are comfortable with are accepting a partial solution.

There is a better way you can do this. I'm going to reframe and reimagine a better approach to short-term rentals than relying on insurance. Simply, insurance is not the right tool to deal with 99% of short-term rental risk. The risk you face is controllable, preventable and defendable. That is the beauty of risk management, and this is not just going to save you money, it's going to make you a new revenue stream, it's going to stop parties, prevent damage and keep your owners happier.

Risk Management

All of us think of ourselves as rational beings, even in times of crisis, applying the laws of reason, risk and probability in a cool and calculated fashion to the choices that confront us. We like to believe we are above average in skills, intelligence, foresight, experience and leadership. Who admits to being an incompetent driver, or a person with anything except a sense of style and sophistication? When are pink shorts or a crinkled linen shirt not appropriate? Yet how realistic are such images? Not everyone can be above average. Furthermore, the most important decisions we make usually occur under complex, confusing, or stressed conditions when you are at your lowest ebb, tired, hungry and grumpy. This is compounded when you look at how the tools we use to find guests are getting even more complex and linked to a widely distributed system of thousands of different booking channels.

Relying on our gut as our forecasting method of choice is only going to end in one way: disaster. We must put aside our complacency and arrogance, we are not infallible, we are human beings whose biggest weakness is our belief that we can conquer nature. If we can overcome that massive elephant and get to a place of logic and rational thought, then our understanding of risk will enable us to make decisions rationally and not emotionally. Suzanne Massie, an American scholar, met with Ronald Reagan many times while he was president of the United States between 1984 and 1987. She taught him the Russian proverb "Doveryai, no proveryai" (Доверяй, но проверяй) meaning "trust, but verify". This sits at the heart of our approach to risk management.

Risk management guides us over a vast range of decision-making, from choosing whether to accept one-night bookings to allowing more guests to stay overnight, from accepting a guest with no reviews to planning where to onboard a new listing, from paying insurance premiums to performing 'know your guest' checks. Risk management in a nutshell is how human beings recognise and respond to the probabilities that we confront. This is what risk management and decision-making are all about and where the balance between controls, measurement and actions are key. It's worth noting that reducing uncertainty has historically been an expensive business, but it is not anymore.

Now, I'm not trying to give you a history lesson but it's amusing to think that, for some, they hold the real beliefs that the future is merely down to the whim of the gods, and that men and women are simply passive before nature. That the future is a mirror of the past or the murky domain of oracles, soothsayers or in our case OTAs who hold the monopoly over knowledge of anticipated events. I can promise you that this is not the case. How great your next guests will be is not decided by the deities living in the sky or the OTAs from where the booking has come from. Risk is a choice rather than a fate. It is something that we have control over. We are free to make choices, it is these choices and actions that we dare to take, which will determine part of our future. For every property manager, this has to be one of the most liberating and peace-giving thoughts.

But why can we not rely on the OTAs to keep us safe? Doesn't Airbnb, Vrbo and Booking.com do this? Well, yes and no. Background checks are used by OTAs to lightly screen guests, to confirm emails are valid and phone numbers work. In the best cases, they will see if the guest has a criminal record. But there are a few problems with this. Most of these checks are expensive if obtainable in the first place. Most importantly, they rely on the guest providing their actual legal identity. While these light checks can put minds at rest and provide a minimal barrier to entry, they're next to useless when it comes to anticipating which guests might engage in antisocial behaviour, and incompetent for professional criminals using false identities. The wrong guests, undetectable through OTA checks, are the reason hosts and property managers unwittingly put their property at risk. I know because it happened to me. Please don't let it happen to you.

These OTA checks are like a colander, they will catch only the dimmest witted of potential abusers whilst letting many predators slip through. Background checks like this help OTAs to appear responsible to local policy makers and can help to ease concerns for hosts, but let's not kid ourselves, these checks are first and foremost a marketing tool designed to suck us into a feeling of safety. Only by performing more in-depth guest screening can you confidently prevent these guests from taking advantage of your property, but if you put the right measures in place, you'll be able to accept last-minute reservations with confidence. More importantly, this change in approach and mindset makes not only accepting direct bookings the safest way to have guests to stay, but it is going to provide those guests with the best possible guest experience. This is before mentioning the benefits of maximising your occupancy rates and revenue.

Why doesn't OTA verification work? Or... How 'Know Your Guest' was created.

Guests don't have 'criminal' stamped on their short-term rental profiles or identity cards. They also don't have 'antisocial', 'troublemaker' or 'on parole'. It's also a deeply unhelpful quirk that hiding behind an alias is particularly easy. Alexander Hughes could be Alex Hughs, Xander Hues, Andy Hugh, A. H., Alexi Hugs or any combination of those plus many more. This is all an aside, though...

Now, my properties are all right next to my home. We converted a barn and love having people to stay on our farm. I mean, love is a strong word, but it pays for my kids to attend an amazing school and supports my family, so it's a wonderful thing in the round. I had a guest to stay through a prominent platform. The guest was ID verified, and looked brilliant with one positive review. I thought great, my gut said fine, and so we went right ahead. They booked for one person, it's a three-bed, so I asked if it was just them and they said yes. Then, on the day, they told me a few more were coming. I mean, no problem, but when they arrived I could just sense something was wrong. They were unloading crates of booze, gas canisters and balloons. They were chucking cigarettes into the garden and being loud and unthoughtful to our other guests.

Being a little glib, I put guests into three buckets: brilliant, fine and tricky. Tricky guests cause problems and quite frankly having them to stay feels like being killed by a thousand cuts. They harm business, they complain about everything from the wrong kind of washing detergent to knocking a table over, smashing the top and then blaming us for having it there. They never leave a good review, and we wouldn't wish to host them again, but do you know what, they are okay, you just need to roll with them.

But this verified individual stood out and it wasn't until 1am that I realised something had gone horrendously wrong. Our other guests had called the police after hearing threats, furniture being thrown and people fighting. The man who made the booking was literally beating up the girls in his party. He then refused to give his details to the police, his name was an alias like the ones above, so his profile name was no help. The police took his fingerprints and then three hours later they returned with eight police cars and a squadron of officers to arrest him.

All I could think the next morning was, why had these guys been allowed to stay with me? Why would someone known to the police not have been flagged by the OTA? That is what started my journey towards building a more intelligent tool and not one built for marketing.

Great risk management can be more than the sum of the parts. Done properly, it's the arena in which we can transform the perception of risk from chance of loss into opportunity for gain, from fate to sophisticated technology that gives meaningful insights of the future, and from helplessness into choice. It also provides an answer that demonstrates to owners that you understand, are on top of and are in control of what is going to happen to their property, and this is key to winning new inventory. It's also important for the industry as we all owe each other a duty of care. We are all responsible for keeping short-term rentals safe from the predators.

Do not think that the past determines the future because it does not. Yes, it can inform the future, it can help quantify the future, but because the future is an unknown, it does not and we will not allow it to determine it. This is why we have built technology to scrutinise what happened in the past to create likely models of what will happen in the future. Patterns of the past can inform us as to what the future may be like, but this is just one data set. It is just one layer that sits alongside multiple other layers that detect how guests interact with screening, whether they screen grab or delay, whether they whizz through or ignore. We are not prisoners of an inevitable future of the wrong guests coming to stay. Risk, combined with risk management, makes us free. Insurance has nothing to do with hosting, changing sheets, making sure the shower drains properly and the guests have the correct arrival instructions. It has nothing to do with blindly accepting any and every guest to stay. It is not about relying on our hangry gut instincts. We are not obliged to accept the spin of the roulette wheel or the cards we are dealt, we are free souls. Our decisions matter. We can change the odds to work in our favour. This gives us the greatest chance of winning.

What we know is that by defining a rational process of risk-taking and risk management, we as a team of innovators are able to provide you with a massively important ingredient that will propel your business and guest experience into a world of speed, power, instant verification and sophisticated checks. The decisions you and we make do change our world and our stars. With command of knowing who is really staying in our properties we can build tremendous futures for ourselves and our businesses. You control who stays in your properties, not the OTA deities. We can also design great bridges between short-term rentals and local communities, between regulation and innovation, between unknowns and taming risk. We can tell you where the bombs are and where they will land so you, and the elephants, will be saved.

Watch an exclusive video with Superhog at **bookdirectblueprint.com**

THE
BOOK DIRECT
BLUEPRINT

Enjoying the book so far?

Leave a review on
Amazon and send proof to
info@boostly.co.uk
for a special (bonus) training!

TECHNOLOGY SIMPLIFIES AND COMPLICATES SHORT–TERM RENTALS

JOHN AN – TECHTAPE

The Journey into Short–Term Rentals

Short-term rental is not a new industry, it has been around for millennia. Some even say the first recorded instance of short-term rentals was the barn where Jesus was born! However, the advent of technology to connect travellers with property owners and managers has transformed short-term rentals into a very easy industry to get into. Simply list a property onto an online travel agency (OTA) such as Airbnb, Vrbo, Booking.com, etc., and soon, guests start booking, and the OTAs take care of the difficult tasks of attracting guests, payment processing, etc. Fundamentally, this business is very simple – connect travellers with property owners/managers and provide a great experience! Communicate with guests, clean the properties and get them ready for guests to check in and enjoy their stay, meet the guests at check-in and provide some personal touches, and then when the guests check out, repeat the process. In fact, this is so simple, the goal quickly shifts from bringing in some ancillary income to adding more properties to multiply the income stream. What can be so difficult about that, right?

Pretty soon, the one property grows to five, then to ten, and then soon, the business has taken over every waking (and sleeping) moment of your life. Constantly tied to your phone to respond to guest messages, not able to take a vacation because you need to be nearby, and not able to enjoy watching a movie in a theatre because your phone is buzzing constantly! The business model of a short-term rental business is extremely simple, but there are many, many moving parts, and without solid underlying systems and processes, growth can only be linear. Each new property requires about the same incremental amount of time/work to run, and quickly becomes unmanageable. And so starts the journey to finding the perfect software that will solve all your problems and do everything for you. How difficult can it be to find software that solves all your problems?

Quest for the Perfect Software to Get Your Life Back

There is lots of property management software (PMS) available (as of this writing, over 500 different options around the world), each one promising that it is the be-all and end-all solution to solve all your short-term rental woes. The list of features and capabilities run pages long. Integrations with multiple OTAs, automated guest messaging, cleaning team management, direct booking website capabilities, smart-lock automation, guest screening, guidebook and upsell, owner portal, metrics and analytics, the list goes on and on and on. Each demo with the sales department convinces you that their software is the be-all and end-all solution to all your problems. And if a feature you ask about is not currently part of the software, they assure you that it is coming in three-to-six months. (Pro-tip: NEVER believe that a feature is almost ready, that's just a ploy by the salesperson to earn their commission by getting you to sign up.)

After selecting one PMS and putting in the time and energy to onboard your properties, some features address some immediate problems, but then other features are either missing, or don't work the way you anticipated, and through the process of onboarding, you realise the software is not everything you were led to believe by the salesperson. But the software works well enough, and the thought of going through onboarding onto another software is daunting. So, you convince yourself that the software works enough, you accept all the shortcomings of it, and just live with it as you continue to grow your business.

If you're 'adventurous', then you may try switching your PMS one or two times, in search of the be-all and end-all PMS that works for YOUR business. This time around, you ask multiple colleagues what they use, and go through a more structured demo process, creating spreadsheets of feature-list comparisons, and asking more questions during the product demos. After careful deliberation, you select the new software, and work through the transition from the old software to the new one. Experiencing hiccups and glitches along the way, over months of working with the new software, the transition is completed. Some of the new features you wanted in the new software work well, but... a feature from the previous software that worked perfectly well is no longer working the way you need – the implementation of that feature is completely different, and so now, this feature that used to work is completely broken for YOUR business! But given the time and energy it takes to transition software, you decide you'll just have to accept broken features, and just live with what you have.

This is a constantly recurring theme in the short-term rental industry, yet each operator believes their experience is unique. I had the tenacity to repeat the process of changing PMS fifteen times (maybe I'm just a slow learner) in search of the unicorn all-in-one software that will work the way I need it to run my short-term rental business. With each new software, the hope and promise of finding my be-all and end-all solution was quickly dashed away, as a given feature would change dramatically with each new software.

Thus began the journey to create a solution that is now TechTape.

Creating Your Cocktail of STR Technology

There are many moving parts in running a short-term rental business. And with each moving part, there are multiple companies providing potential solutions to help facilitate the business operations. Whether it be for guest communication, dynamic pricing, guest screening and verification, smart locks and access control, guidebooks and upsell platforms, direct booking websites, channel management, cleaning and maintenance management, the list goes on and on and on. And, of course, there are too many property management systems (over 500 and growing at the time of this writing). There is no shortage of technology options to help address almost any challenge faced by a short-term rental business. And with so many options for each specific challenge, the solution provided by one software provider may be perfect for one operator, while the same software may not fit the needs of another. The great news is that there are lots of options to pick and choose from to find the software that meets YOUR specific business needs.

On the flip side, having so many options not only means that there are many options to wade through and evaluate, it also means many of the different software packages may not be integrated. Often, the selection of the software for your business is dictated more by the integrations decisions made by the software provider, and less on whether the software truly meets YOUR business needs. Yet again, short-term rental operators settle for a mix of technologies that doesn't quite meet their business needs. Yet it works better than alternative options, so this becomes the status quo.

TechTape takes a surgical approach to identifying the key core technologies that meet most of the needs of YOUR business, and then build out workflows and dashboards with ancillary software that work for YOUR business. This is a semi-customised approach to take the best-in-class available products, and create smooth workflows and dashboards so these disparate technologies all work together!

Approach to Selecting the PMS

The PMS is the core of any tech stack for a short-term rental business. The PMS should be the central system of truth that helps keep everything organised. But because there are so many options available, simply selecting this core software itself is a challenge. When I started out, I asked around to get recommendations from colleagues. What I discovered was that even the operators who seemed to understand the industry did not have a good handle on the software and technologies, and often, their recommendations caused me time and money trying software that didn't work for my business. Moreover, often shortly after I received their recommendation and onboarded onto a new PMS, I noticed that they had switched their software! What I learned from this experience was that a software platform that works for one operator often is not good for another operator, and basing software selection on recommendations is no better than simply trying software without any recommendations.

Because there are so many different features and functions that PMS could provide, it is incredibly challenging to compare generic feature lists between competing platforms. For most features, it comes down to the details of how a software provider decided to implement them. For example, when I was on my journey of switching from one PMS to another, each time I switched, I was pursuing the shiny new feature that I wanted but didn't necessarily need. At a certain point, I was using a PMS, and it was working well enough for me and my business; it had robust guest messaging, it was integrated with the dynamic pricing software I needed to use, it was connected to Airbnb, Vrbo and Booking.com. It had a direct booking website. It even had a mobile app, but the mobile app was limited to showing the calendar and sending basic messages. The overall PMS was very capable, but I wanted a fully functional mobile app, one that enabled me to perform all functions that I could when I was sitting in front of a computer. Because of this one desire, I decided to scrap the whole PMS and search for another one that had a fully functional mobile app.

After a lengthy search process, and an even lengthier transition from the previous PMS to the new one, I was very happy that the new one had a fully functional mobile app. However, some of the basic features I had grown accustomed to with my previous PMS just didn't work quite right for my business. For example, the new PMS advertised that it had a direct booking website feature. But while my previous PMS allowed me to choose my own domain, the new one only allowed me to select from a handful of domain names offered by the PMS! The addition of getting a fully mobile app came with the inadvertent loss of my direct booking website! Comparing a list of features assured me that the new PMS would have a direct booking website, but little did I realise that the implementation of this feature would be so drastically different that it was essentially useless!

I was pursuing a unicorn all-in-one solution, and I thought that, through a careful comparison of the features, I would be able to find the right PMS. But, after repeated experiences like the story mentioned above, I slowly came to the conclusion that the unicorn all-in-one solution does not exist, and cannot exist because the implementation of features between similar software is often drastically different.

How to Put Together a Tech Stack

Just because the unicorn all-in-one software for your business doesn't exist does not mean that all is lost. There is method and process to building out the right tech stack. The first and most important step is understanding and accepting the truth that there is no unicorn software solution that meets all your business needs.

With that as a starting point, the first decision to make in selecting a PMS is the key channels that are most important and critical to your business, and then ONLY evaluate PMS that have tight integration with the channels. This helps to minimise the number of PMS that need to be evaluated. If a PMS doesn't integrate with your key channel, just don't include it in the pool of potential software. Of course, there are always dedicated channel managers that enable connection to many different channels. However, the connectivity made through a channel manager often does not provide the full integration and automation, particularly guest messaging, and so creates challenging workflows that require more manual interventions to make work properly. For niche channels, the additional workflow may be tolerable. However, for the key channels that are the core of your business, you want all the integrations to work smoothly.

Then, determine the top three-to-four features that are most important to you and your business. Not a long laundry list, but just the top three or four. Of course, basic functionality of automated messaging and calendar management are expected. So, other features outside of the basic functionality. For instance, for me, my top features were: 1) fully functional mobile application; 2) direct booking website with ability to use custom domain name; 3) have a robust API (application programming interface) and webhook capabilities to allow integrations.

Then, you can compare pricing and terms of the software. While reducing the cost is, of course, important, paying less for a solution that doesn't work quite right is worse than paying more for a software that works. I am, of course, very price sensitive, but the right tool is more important than saving money. Once these two steps are followed, the number of software options gets whittled down into a small subset of viable options.

Then, there will be some features of the PMS that also work for your business, and some features that don't work well. This is normal and expected, and at this point, don't fall for the temptation to switch PMS because of some features that don't work well for your business. There is no perfect unicorn, and changing again will introduce different problems.

This is where TechTape can create solutions that help complete out the additional needs and features that are important for your business. TechTape can help identify the core additional business needs and build out semi-customised solutions that fill them out. For some managers, it may be an ability to create an online guest information form, or a digital product payment processing, or automatic lock code generation, or a semi-customised dashboard that provides a high-level overview of the business that brings in information from different software/platforms. TechTape provides consultation to help understand the needs, and then builds out the most important features that complement the core PMS's feature set.

The approach TechTape takes is to use all off-the-shelf software and technologies, and find ways to integrate these tools, all using no-code processes and workflows. TechTape then maintains these systems, while the property manager has a fully functional workflow and dashboard. The name TechTape derives from duct tape, and so TechTape is capable of 'taping' together different technologies to make it work.

One of the benefits of this approach is that semi-customised solutions can be implemented with a quick turnaround time. These solutions can be implemented and operational in days or weeks. And, if there are some refinements required, iterations are also very fast. So, while software development takes months to years to implement, TechTape's solutions become operational much quicker.

The approach TechTape takes can be compared to buying a suit. TechTape creates a semi-custom solution by utilising all existing products, and then customising how the technologies work together. TechTape does not create custom software, which would be the equivalent of buying a fully tailored suit. Such an approach would be incredibly expensive, and would involve long timeframes. Simply using existing software without TechTape is equivalent to purchasing an off-the-rack suit, which does not quite fit properly. Instead, TechTape's approach is very similar to purchasing a semi-custom suit, where most of the components and pieces are ready to go, but a few measurements are customised. The result is a suit that fits very well but is less expensive than a custom suit and can be produced in a shorter timeframe.

Closing Thoughts

The journey I experienced with STR technology is very common and almost every property manager experiences the same problem. Each new property manager repeats this problem, experiences it, settles on a tech, and then moves on. The amount of time and energy wasted across the entire industry is tremendous. I continue to see property managers who embark on this frustrating and time-wasting journey. TechTape's goal is to help save time, money and aggravation across the short-term rental industry. Many veterans in the industry are already operating with a tech stack that doesn't quite work well for them, but have resigned themselves to continue to accept their pain points. Many new entrants into the industry believe that a unicorn software exists.

Head to **bookdirectblueprint.com** for an exclusive interview with John An.

YOUR RECIPE FOR ETERNAL GUEST LOYALTY

TOUCH STAY

You're cautiously wending your way down a shadowy London mews. In the daytime, it's a beautiful microcosm of the city's charms: historic buildings and cobbled streets. At night, with limited street lighting and a confined space, it makes for an eerie approach for newcomers.

As if this wasn't enough, it's the end of a long day. It's close to midnight, and the only thing you want now is a warm, comfy bed. Instead, you're fumbling about outside your short-term rental, desperately looking for a key box or an electronic door lock. Anything that might give a hint as to how you access the property. But… nothing. You're stuck outside, unable to overcome the final yet vital hurdle of a locked front door.

And, more than that, it doesn't feel safe. You're in a large city, in an area you don't know well, at the bottom of a quiet, dingy street. So, you switch on the car headlights to search. The neighbours probably won't be a fan of this, but that's your last concern right now. Still, you can't see anything.

As a final resort, you call the property manager's support line. It rings, and rings, and rings… Until, joy of joys, someone finally picks up! They tell you there's a key box hidden in a small cupboard on the side wall. After a few more minutes of searching, you're finally able to slide into bed.

Stressful situation resolved. But would you book another property managed by that company and risk a similar thing happening again?

Prioritise Guest Communication. Prioritise Your Business.

This was an actual experience that Andy, Touch Stay's CEO, had whilst travelling. It demonstrated a theme he'd been noticing for a while: holiday rental hosts and managers were struggling to communicate with guests.

Hosts were passionate about providing a wonderful experience but had so much on their plates that crucial information – such as where the key box was located – was slipping through the cracks.

Proactive communications are an integral part of your direct booking toolkit. Serve guests the information they need, when they need it, with a sprinkling of your personal touch, and you'll reclaim time in your day whilst waving off happy guests. These visitors will leave five-star reviews and propel their peers straight to your direct booking site.

The formula is simple: prepared guests + relaxed hosts = smiles all round!

How (Not) to Nail Guest Communications

Let's start with an example of what *not* to do. The following experience of guest communications, shared on Touch Stay's podcast by Nokori founder Wes Melton, stands out for all the wrong reasons.

Wes had taken a work-cation to the beach in North Carolina and had chosen a rental property that would suit his working intent and his family's need for entertainment.

However, when Wes tried to find something for his kids to watch, he noticed a sign next to the television: "$150 fine for using Netflix".

The property manager may have had one too many experiences of visitors forgetting to log out, or muddling the TV settings, but they were channelling their frustration into aggressive notes. They were communicating with their guests as though they were a hassle.

Whilst clearly conveying your house rules is a key element of your guest communications, this needs to be done respectfully. Plastering hostile notes all over your property is guaranteed to make your guests feel unwelcome.

Listen to The Guest Cast at touchstay.com/podcast to hear in Wes's own words how this host's belligerent signage affected his stay.

Craft Successful Guest Communications

In contrast, if you can make them feel at home, informed and prepared at every stage of their journey with you, then you'll wave goodbye to a guest who will advocate for you far and wide.

Instead, implement energised, proactive communications before, during and after their stay.

How to set clear expectations

From properties that haven't been cleaned, to properties that don't actually exist, there are plenty of horror stories to make travellers wary.

Reassure guests with communications that set clear, accurate expectations:

- Use your direct booking site and/or listing to showcase numerous clear photos of your property.
- Craft coherent, engaging website copy.
- Convey crucial property information and tell guests exactly where they can find it.
- Outline your house rules from the get-go.
- Share an insight into your local area.

- Inspire them to explore beyond your front door.

The more detail you can include, the better. Show guests they can trust you with coherent, in-depth information.

Guests do read! But don't be afraid to repeat yourself

Just because you send guests the essential information they need, this doesn't mean they'll absorb it on first view. You could send them answers to every single FAQ, and they might still arrive looking lost and confused because they didn't engage with your access instructions.

So, in the lead up to their arrival, serve them the crucial information they need multiple times, and in various formats. People like to consume information in different ways. Some will get stuck into a long-form email, whilst others will barely skim a quick text. Hit every type of guest by using a variety of forms of communication: email, SMS, WhatsApp, even snail mail.

Strike the right tone in your house rules

You need your house rules to be clear from the off. Your guests need to know:

- What you expect of them, and what they can expect of you.
- If there will be consequences for broken rules.
- What the consequences will be, and how you'll communicate them.

Rather than plastering antagonistic Post-it notes around the property, as Wes Melton's host did, put your rules front and centre in your pre-arrival communications and guest welcome book, and keep your tone clear and respectful. This way, your requirements are clearly presented and accessible, but they don't intrude unnecessarily on your guest's experience.

Be honest about what you have

Karen Beddow, creator of Mini Travellers, told our podcast listeners how she arrived at one holiday property to discover that the wall-mounted television she'd seen in photos did exist, but couldn't be plugged in. Technically, the property owner hadn't lied, but that didn't alter Karen's disappointment.

Exaggerating your property's plus points might feel like a good way to attract more guests at a higher price point, but all it really does is guarantee disillusioned guests who leave negative reviews.

Be upfront about your property's pros and cons on your website and in your pre-arrival communications.

- Is there construction happening nearby? Acknowledge it, be clear on the proximity, and state that you have adjusted the price to reflect it.
- Are there trains or other traffic? Be specific on the frequency and volume, and explain how you mitigate any noise.

Clear initial communications put you in a great position to exceed your guests' expectations, which always makes for a glowing review.

Retain your brand voice

Your guests want to know that they're communicating with a real human being, not a computer. Injecting some personality into your messages strengthens the personal connection that you build with visitors, which is crucial to establishing long-lasting relationships.

At the same time, tailor the tone and content of your emails to your target guest. If you know you get a lot of family reunions organised by older relatives, filling your emails with Gen Z slang won't help them to connect with you.

If you're using message scheduling, make sure that your message templates contain short codes (or merge tags) that personalise them to each guest. This could be as simple as a code that inserts the guest's first name into the greeting.

Small touches like this are easy to set up and make a serious difference to how your guests feel. Alissa Cincotta, the very first guest on our podcast, noted the huge impact it had when she and her husband went on their honeymoon and every employee at their hotel greeted them by name. Years later, she's still talking about that experience. Learning and using your guests' names is a simple, scalable way to make them feel special.

To Guest Loyalty and Beyond!

Let's look at crucial communication touch points throughout the guest experience.

Marketers often use a model called a customer journey infinity loop – we're going to call it the *guest* journey infinity loop. Take a look at the following diagram.

The guest journey infinity loop contains six stages, all connected in a constant flow:

- Awareness – a potential guest first comes across your property.
- Consideration – they mull over whether they'd like to book a stay.
- Purchase – they book in for a few nights.
- Anticipation – they get inspired by your recommendations and obvious professionalism.
- Advocacy – they love their time with you and rave about you to everyone they know.
- Loyalty – they return again and again, and continue to

spread the word.

Once a guest has completed the "purchase" stage of the loop, this is your opportunity to set and exceed their expectations. If you can make their stay everything they dreamed it would be (and more!), then you'll wave goodbye to a guest who will advocate for your offering in:

- The review they write.
- The way they describe their holiday to friends and family.
- The photos and captions they share on social media.
- The notes they leave for other guests in your guestbook.

As a world-renowned photographer, Alissa Cincotta had many travel stories to share on our podcast. During one particularly memorable trip to Italy, her vacation rental host offered her and her husband a private wine tasting in the cool depths of his wine cellar. Alissa returned home with a small bottle of limoncello that reminds her of her stay every time she sees it.

This host provided everything Alissa had been hoping for – and more! As a result, she's told this story over and over again, including every time a visitor comments on her memento. Each potential guest who hears her story enters the "awareness" stage of the guest journey via a trusted source who is already singing this host's praises.

Head to touchstay.com/podcast to hear Alissa explain the impact the simplest gestures can have.

The Power of Online Advocacy

The virtual version of Alissa's in-person advocacy is the online guest review. Exceeding your guests' expectations will earn you reviews such as these who stayed with Touch Stay users:

"Kate was great at communicating with me before the trip, and the online guide to the property was beyond comprehensive. We will certainly keep their place in mind for future trips!" – a guest at The Malthouse

"Nat and Tyann overdeliver on the experience of staying at their property. Before we checked in, we received multiple emails of local recommendations and what to expect, which makes the whole part of getting there stress free. The online website for their guests is amazing!! Definitely will be back!" – a guest at Missouri Haus

"Heather is a fantastic host and communicator, immediately responsive to any question and full of helpful advice. Her phone app is chock full of practical information and ideas of how to spend days and nights. We would rent this house again (and again)." – a guest at Casa Pace e Gioia

Glowing reviews have immense power to add credibility to your direct booking site and social media. 52% of travellers seek out social media recommendations when looking for somewhere to stay (Bookfull: https://bookfull.com/2018/02/01/vacation-rental-statistics/), and if your pages are packed full of five-star reviews from happy guests, that's proof right there that you're a stellar host.

How to communicate guest reviews to drive direct bookings:

- Social media activity: posts, stories, carousels, clips from your guestbook, etc.
- Add them to your book direct website.
- Pop one in your email footer.
- Include a different one in each email newsletter.

If you can ace guest communication, prospective guests will enter the "awareness" and "consideration" stages of the guest journey via recommendations from trusted sources. Drive happy guests to your direct booking site and social media channels, have them forward your emails to friends, and they'll become your best marketing assets.

Choreograph Your Communication Flow

Given that your communications are so essential to generating these five-star reviews, adopting a haphazard approach to communicating could quite literally be losing you money.

The time between booking and arrival is fundamental to influencing the guest's experience. This is your chance to establish yourself as the consummate, personable hospitality professional before your guest has even arrived.

"I've stayed in many places all over the world. I have NEVER seen an app guide and so much useful information. My group was completely blown away. Our excitement is now on another level!" – guest at Seattle Vacation Home

"What a great online guide you've put together for the house! We've been renting for more than fifteen years, and this is the best that I've seen. Will definitely read through it." – guest at Our Humble Homes

To get guests this excited for their stay, you need a "contact strategy", or what we more cheerily call a guest communication flow. And one that's proactive, yet efficient for you to manage. The idea being it saves (even regains) you time.

13–Step Guest Communication Flow

Here's a suggested guest communication flow that covers the entirety of a guest's stay:

1. **Post booking confirmation**: make personal contact (especially if they booked via an OTA) and keep in touch.
2. **Essential travel details**: drop a note about insurance and any other key documents.
3. **Intro to the local area:** highlight the best local restaurants, specifying those that need to be booked in advance.
4. **Key arrival info:** serve guests essential access instructions shortly before they set off.
5. **Safe travels:** continue building your personal relationship by wishing guests a safe journey.
6. **Post-arrival check-in:** check they arrived safely and encourage them to raise any concerns.
7. **Practical property details:** spotlight instructions for tricky appliances.
8. **Making the most of their time:** highlight the amenities available.
9. **The nitty-gritty details:** remind them it's rubbish day tomorrow.
10. **Promote your upsells:** nudge them towards your referral link for the nearby spa.
11. **Pre-departure checklist:** remind them of what they need to do before departing.
12. **Review request:** thank guests for staying and tell them how to leave a review.

13. **Keep in touch:** point them towards your social media, email newsletter and direct booking site.

This is just a starting point. Your personal communication flow will also depend on the type of property you own, and how far in advance guests book.

If guests generally book your rental three or four months in advance, you might share essential travel details twice: once shortly after they book, and once a month before their arrival date. If guests tend to book with you at the last minute, you'll only need to send these details once.

Answer Questions Before Guests Ask Them

Communicate proactively and you'll answer questions before your guests even realise they need to ask them. When Hannah, Touch Stay's Creative Media Manager, arrived in Spain after a twenty-four-hour drive, all she wanted was a clean, comfortable place to rest. What she got was a hot, sticky apartment and a dismissive host.

The worst part? It was 35°C (95°F) and there was no air conditioning. Whilst this might have been manageable for her host, who was acclimatised to Spain's soaring temperatures, for Hannah it was unbearable.

You can apply this principle to your practical property information: just because something comes naturally to you, this doesn't mean it will come naturally to a newcomer.

- Does the back door key need a bit of a wiggle to get it to slide in? Tell your guests!

- Does the bathroom tap need to be tightened firmly to be properly 'off'? Tell your guests!
- Does the hot tub lid have to be replaced in a specific way to be safely covered? Tell your guests!

Hannah took to our podcast to explain how, on a separate trip to Cuba, she stayed with a host who took exactly this approach. They realised that, as a woman travelling alone, Hannah might feel more intimidated by the catcalling common to the locality. And so, they warned her that it was likely to happen, and explained that, whilst unpleasant, it wasn't meant aggressively. This put Hannah's mind at ease as soon as she arrived.

Details which might seem small to you will help your guests make the very most of their stay and reduce the number of questions you have to address.

One truly objective way to determine which questions need answering is to ask someone to play at being a guest for you. This could be a friend or a professional hospitality consultant, but it must be someone who doesn't know the place. Invite them to book and stay (fully refunded!) and then constructively feed back to you about the booking, pre-arrival, stay and post-departure experiences.

Don't Let Guests Lose Your Business Card

You need your guests to remember *you*, not the OTA through which they booked. So, your communications should take every opportunity to embed your brand in their memories.

- Add your logo to all communication materials: digital guidebook, email footer, website.

- Make personal contact with guests early and regularly throughout their stay.
- Maintain a consistent, warm tone of voice that lets your brand personality shine through.
- Point guests towards your newsletter, social media and website.

Imbue your communications with your logo, brand colours, and tone of voice to solidify your brand within guests' memories of their stay. Rather than telling friends they stayed in "a wonderful Airbnb" and then struggling to find your listing, they'll send them straight to your direct booking site.

Communicate More. Do Less.

Touch Stay's co-founders, Andy and Joe, designed their digital guidebook software to support guests *and* hosts. Proactive, effective communications allow you to be more present in your guest's experience, whilst actually reclaiming hours in your day.

When you deposit all your information in a polished, accessible digital guidebook, guests can always access the crucial details they need. This means fewer guest questions, and more time for you. In fact, 86% of Touch Stay users more than halve the time they spend managing guests!

Our digital guidebooks are specifically designed to help you tick all the guest communication boxes we list above. It's easy as pie for you to include all your need-to-know practical property information, and to show off the details a guest can experience through videos, pictures and the written word. Plus, we encourage you to wrap up your guidebook by pointing guests to your direct booking site, newsletter sign-up and social media profiles. You can even apply your own logo and brand colours.

And it gets better! Our guest notification system, Memo, helps you to share this information at the exact moment your guests need it most, without you having to lift a finger.

The results? Your guests feel welcomed, prepared and special at every moment throughout their stay. They ask you fewer questions. And you have more time to focus on actually hosting them.

Touch Stay has kindly recorded a walkthrough video on how to set up your digital guidebook for the ultimate guest experience for all **Blueprint** readers. Head to **bookdirectblueprint.com** to find out more.

CORPORATE RENTAL STRATEGIES

ROBERTIN NUNEZ – CO HOST EXPERT COMPANY

I am Robertin Nunez, CEO and co-founder of the Co Host Expert Company and LivingQuarters.net, and board member at Hey Comfort Miami, all part of the Group of Associated Hospitality Companies. I've been in the real estate development and the corporate and entertainment travel industry for over twenty-five years with offices at various times in New York City, Los Angeles, Philadelphia, Madrid and London. We are professional corporate travel, short and mid-term rental property management companies servicing business and leisure travellers around the world in Miami, New York City and Philadelphia. We are also the back-end operations for several short and mid-term management companies in our region who white label our professional management services as we support their management and corporate rental agenda.

Our speciality is providing corporate rental housing to companies and organisations, insurance companies, housing relocation specialists, employee relocation, not-for-profits, military, sports and entertainment industry, and the work from home movement. We also assist short/mid-term rental operators in developing a corporate rental housing plan and strategy to increase their bookings and revenues to become masters of their business revenue stream while reducing their dependency on OTAs.

2,700 Nights Is Your New Normal

I am writing this chapter on corporate rental bookings and housing strategies during the week we closed a 2,700-night corporate housing request within a ninety-day reservation period in one of our property portfolios. The transaction took our team 4.5 days and generated over $200,000 in sales. This reservation further confirms our belief and position in this industry that: **companies and organisations heavily rely on corporate rental housing companies and professionals to fulfil their corporate housing travel needs.** This reservation is one of the many bookings we have worked smart at converting from email request to a major reservation. It also raises the bar at our family of companies to understand that 2,700 nights is the new normal. It's a great accomplishment by our sales and ground operations team, all credit to them. This 2,700-night reservation is not an anomaly, long-term stays taking up 30-70% of operator inventory happen often within this industry, within our businesses, management companies we work with and companies and operators that we know. Corporate clients with consistent housing needs exist in abundance and you, with a concise corporate rental plan and strategy, can realise these kinds of bookings. This chapter is designed to help you analyse:

1. Where is your business in the corporate housing rental space?
2. How to create, implement and execute a corporate booking strategy into your current and future business operations.
3. How to increase your current corporate housing rental revenue.

4. Offer the resources, tips and access to us to help you build this system.

Corporate travel is a term loosely defined in this industry. Many operators consider a corporate travel reservation to be a booking that a business traveller/company makes for their rental property. The scenario plays out like this: the client books a property from the operator via an OTA or a friend's referral, checks in and now the operator believes they are providing business and corporate rental travel services – this is incorrect. And this is also not scalable.

Understanding the Client

"Corporate travel" is a corporation or business conducting business travel. As a short, mid-term or corporate rental housing operator, one must understand that business travellers require a different level of service. The travel coordinators handling the travel needs for their companies are far from your standard OTA leisure guest seeking a cheap deal for a place to stay.

Travel coordinators, some who have been in the industry for over twenty years, are responsible for providing their company and organisation with a reliable and concise travel plan within the scope of their agenda. They answer to CEOs of major companies, corporate executives, clients, high-end clientele, potential new business partners and many other client types. This is why establishing a solid corporate housing travel plan and service is imperative for operators looking to service these clients. You will work with some very experienced people.

The travel coordinator or planner, aka "the client", will relay their corporate housing needs to the operator servicing them. FYI, that in most cases will change. They must feel comfortable knowing that the operator servicing them is an established and experienced operator or company, knows what they are doing within this space and can adjust to changes and situations as they may arise within their reservations. TRUST and COMFORT are imperative to establish early on.

OTAs do make it easier for some company staff members to use these online companies. Yet there are many companies, especially the more established ones, that will NOT use an OTA to seek housing for their staff members during their business travels. The liabilities they face when booking unknown properties from unknown operators on an OTA are too high for them to consider. The "direct contact information" blocks set in place by the OTAs further hinders establishing the TRUST factor between the client and yourself. You need a proven and strategic process to establish a system within your company and organisation to mediate this and help you excel in the corporate rental housing space. Let's dive in!

IT'S ALL SALES: To establish or grow a corporate rental housing system, housing operators must understand that one thing alone leads to the increase of reservations and revenue with business travel clients – **and that is sales**. Corporate travel thrives when you convert requests into confirmed reservations/sales. There is a shortage of new travel companies and operators offering corporate travel services because many have replaced direct sales, relationship and client communications with features like "Instant Book". Many operators fear having to actually promote and sell their service and inventory to a client. Some operators are simply not aware, unless you are reading this. Now you are aware! The OTAs make it so easy and possible for operators to leave the sales and bookings in the hands of a third party. They handle everything for a fee, which has created a "take it easy" approach with operators on developing in-house sales strategies to draw in corporate booking clients.

3–Step Approach Corporate Clients Use When Seeking Corporate Housing

1. Destination – where do we NEED to be? It's business, so it's a NEED!
2. What is our budget? Cost matters!
3. What is the best, most reliable option for what we are spending? Quality for what the clients pay is a priority!

A Professional Website: detailing your services, speciality market and contact information is critical. If a potential client can't find or contact you then you don't exist to them. And when they find you, make sure what they find appeals to a business traveller seeking your services. When creating your website:

a. Do not over clutter it with details – be concise.

b. Have professional photos of your inventory.

c. Accurate up-to-date contact information.

d. Have automated responses set up for client requests that includes scheduling a time to speak and/or follow up with them. TIP – have well written autoresponders prompting those who contact you to stay in touch and that you will get back to them during business hours.

e. Keep it simple, clean and right to the point.

f. Have your site professionally edited for grammar.

g. Establish credibility by listing any organisations, accreditations or memberships you may have within this space.

h. Connect your site to your social media (clean up your social media).

i. Real-time property inventory availability is advised but you can also leave property calendars open, so you can offer the client another property they didn't initially consider. This happens within our organisation on a daily basis. Client reaches out for one thing, it's not available and we wind up closing them on another property that is available. This is where your sales skills come in. Don't worry, we can help you with that.

j. PLEASE FOLLOW UP for all requests, even if you do not have the availability.

k. LINKEDIN – clients will look you up and corporate clients will most likely look you up on LinkedIn. Make your LinkedIn page an example of your business.

Know Your Market!

VISA WORK PROGRAMMES ARE GREAT FOR CORPORATE BOOKINGS – every destination has a reason travellers visit. Some countries have work visa programmes for work from home travellers or new business startups. This is a great source for corporate travel clients seeking to relocate to another/your market. Ireland, Ecuador, The Netherlands, The Czech Republic, Canada, New Zealand and Australia among a few all have visa programmes for business travellers. Research these programmes and contact the departments in charge. Our experience has found these departments to be supportive of corporate housing operators looking to house the business travellers they are commissioned to draw in. It may be an informal partnership, they are focusing on bringing in the business travellers, you are focused on housing them, it's a logical fit.

"WFH" (Work from Home) has also prompted lovely Caribbean islands to offer creative entrepreneurial and business travel work visa programmes. Business travellers and executives have uprooted, left city and cubicle living and sailed off to the sandy beaches and warm breezes of many of these tropical destinations.

Proven Success: In 2020, during the height of the pandemic, we left city living and relocated to the paradise island of Aruba, set up our operations and it became the think tank for the companies back in the States and abroad. All business decisions and growth moves for the companies in the States were made under a mango tree on the island. CEOs still had to keep their businesses alive while trying to stay alive themselves. We created a four-suite work from home villa for corporate travellers while living in Aruba. It was a huge success, we met great people, they referred other business colleagues and, when the pandemic eased up, we headed back to the States.

Consider where you can potentially enter and benefit from these creative visa programmes that can add to your corporate travel business. Here are a few examples:

1. **Aruba** is offering its "One Happy Workation" programme, which allows US remote workers to live and work in Aruba for up to ninety days, as long as they have a US passport.
2. **Curaçao** – The new "@HOME in Curaçao" programme is designed to "extend the length of stay on the island for remote workers", and other long-stay candidates, including investors.

3. **Montserrat** has announced its Remote Workers Stamp. The twelve-month, long-distance work visa will give professionals and entrepreneurs an opportunity to trade in a routine at-home workplace for black sand beaches and cultural offerings.

4. **The Bahamas** offers the **B**ahamas **E**xtended **A**ccess **T**ravel **S**tay (BEATS) programme. The one-year residency permit is designed to allow professionals and students to work or study remotely from The Bahamas.

There are many more islands that offer similar business and corporate travel work visas. Contact us and we can help you identify a corporate rental housing plan for your current or considered destination.

In Your Backyard: Companies headquartered in your area are an abundant source for corporate travel bookings. These companies have vendors, potential clients, company events and staff members travelling into their headquarters. Contact these companies and inform them that you can assist them with their local business travel needs.

A Gold Mine! Visitor centres and convention centres for your area are partly created to welcome and draw in business travellers and major events. They have a calendar of upcoming events, and when you do further research you can locate the companies coming into town and offer your property inventory. And continue reaching out until the week of the event, as many companies book on short notice.

Proven Success: In 2017-2018 we contacted an organisation that organised a large holiday trade fair for vendors and exhibitors. After two calls and the correct strategic questions, they connected us to the person who was in charge of housing for the vendors. Currently she was overwhelmed with finding a housing solution for vendors. And it was as if our call was right on time. She referred us to a few of the vendors and we wound up closing out six vendors for an average of forty-five nights each = 270 nights. And some of them returned the next year and booked with us.

The SBA or organisations that help bring in businesses to your region are a great source of leads. Build a relationship or contacts within these organisations and come up with creative offers for businesses looking to travel or relocate to your city.

Housing Relocation Specialists are a major source of business. Most major cities and regions have companies who specialise in providing housing for business travellers. Locate who these companies are and introduce your company, service and inventory to them. Note, some of these companies' main source of business is housing corporate and business travellers. They need inventory and they also are comfortable working with reliable housing providers for their clients' housing needs. Become that provider.

Real Estate Offices who manage properties at times have emergency requests, sometimes after business hours (YOUR WEBSITE HELPS HERE) and can range from one to 180+ nights. Contact them and offer them a realtor discount of 10% for all direct bookings they make.

Insurance Relocation Companies must service their clients in need of emergency housing due to crisis or emergency. Fires, natural disasters and/or property damages are some of the reasons that insurance relocation companies must find safe, adequate and reliable housing for their clients.

Military Personnel can be a major short and mid-term housing client. Many families relocate due to their military assignments. Although the military provides housing, there is a time when the families are in transition, providing you with the opportunity to service a reliable paying client – the government – for the time they are in need. I also suggest you offer a military discount and honour those who serve your country.

The Travel Nurse/Health Care Sector. In the United States, travel nursing is a robust industry where nurses are booking housing for an average of thirteen weeks in other cities while on their work contracts within the care industries. They are also offered extensions and may rebook with you for another possible thirteen weeks. One travel nurse contract can provide you with 25%-50% of your yearly bookings. We have significant data in the United States to help you locate viable travel nurse markets and how to service this market and would be happy to assist you.

Consolidate Your Efforts — Work the Floor

Register with CHPA Corporate Housing Providers Association and similar Corporate Housing Relocation Conferences. Attend the annual and local regional events and become familiar with where and how corporate business travellers are booking and being serviced. These conferences provide a wealth of contacts, such as housing providers, vendors and companies all servicing the same industry of corporate travel.

Procedures

An operator must have a standard procedure on how to service a request and process a reservation for corporate housing travellers.

1. Professional email: represent your company professionally. If

you are not a company, then select a professional email that shows you are a serious operator in your space.

2. Voicemail: if the travel coordinator for a large group of Apple executives contacted you and was sent to your voicemail, what would they hear? Make your voicemail a professional representation of you and your company. And make sure to check it and instruct callers to email or text you.

3. Requests: corporate travellers will make requests and sometimes the request is not as specific as you'd like it to be. This is a great opportunity to contact the person making the request and open the lines of communication to find out more about their request, their needs and their company. If you handle this correctly and ask the right questions, you will have exactly what you need to have the next conversation and lead your way to closing the sale/reservation.

Respond Quickly and Lead them to Book

Business has a sense of urgency. Consider that the client did not only contact you or only consider your property. Believe there's another operator out there submitting a response to this same request. The first response with the information requested has a higher chance of closing the request.

Follow Up

I cannot emphasise enough how important FOLLOW UP is. One reason many corporate reservations are missed opportunities is because operators do not follow up with the request. Do not assume because they didn't contact you back that they are not interested. Clients may have a lot on their plate, organising their travels, families, current life and business matters. Their housing needs are important, yet you must take the lead and follow up with them and let them know you are here to make the decision to use your service and book your property with a smooth transaction.

"Hi Susan, this is Robertin, just checking to see if you liked the properties we sent you and if your dates have changed? I'm here to assist, thank you."

The second part of the first sentence leads the potential client to respond. And if they don't respond, follow up again.

Once you are in the closing stages of the booking and you have successfully wooed the client, dig deeper. Find out how, where, why and how often they travel and if they have anything else coming up. If you are performing in a stellar mode, the client is more likely to share details of their future travel agendas, which leads to more potential reservations.

Invoicing – The client books directly through you. There are hundreds of invoicing systems out there that make you look like the professional you are or want to be, pick one. Skynova is a good invoicing system and it's free for smaller client needs.

REVIEW YOUR INVOICE: Review your invoice carefully. Once sent, chances are you will not be able to edit or add on any expense you may have missed.

STELLAR SERVICE: If there's an issue at the property, something out of your control, handle it. What is in your control is the quality of the service you provide the client in response. If there is an issue, especially early on, before or during check in, be 100% committed to helping the client through the process and find a quick professional resolution.

Additional Revenue Models for Corporate Travellers

There are many profitable avenues to explore. Our 2700-night corporate clients were in a bind, so we stepped in to assist. We assisted the client with their logistical parking needs. We located a local parking lot and negotiated a set rate for twenty-four spaces for ninety days, and offered the parking spaces with a modest mark up to the client. The client was very pleased that we solved their parking problem and happily paid the invoice in full, earning us an additional $7,200.

Guest Expectation Quality Control: This is one of the most important parts of this corporate travel chapter. We have a pre-inspection and response team ready for all corporate bookings. The client mentioned above had three major move-in dates. Knowing this, we scheduled our team to be on call and available on those dates for any and all matters that needed to be resolved for the client. And there were calls and we did respond quickly and professionally.

Our pre-inspection team checked each unit prior to check-in. Even with that, the client still contacted us for several of their staff members who found issues at their units. These weren't issues missed by our pre-inspection team, these were issues based on guest expectations or not reading check-in instructions. Quickly, professionally and kindly, we responded to each request and provided a resolution to the matter. This is in line with our motto to have STELLAR service for our business clients.

Client Testimonial: "You and your team have been great and we appreciate your quick response to our concerns. By the way, do you service other markets? I am going to refer you to a colleague of mine who is overseeing a major company event." SUCCESS!

There is so much more for our company to offer when creating and designing an amazing corporate travel strategy for our clients, yet we had only one chapter to bring you up to speed and I hope we brought some light to this amazing and lucrative sector of this short/mid-term and corporate travel industry. I hope my and my team's experience provided you with an understanding of how important corporate travel can be to the success of your housing portfolio and also how profitable it can be.

And let's discuss how to get your corporate housing booking system and business up and thriving.

To watch an exclusive interview with Robertin Nunez head to **bookdirectblueprint.com**

YOU'VE DONE THE GROUNDWORK

NOW IT'S TIME TO LAY THE FOUNDATIONS

Over the last couple of hundred pages, you've been in the company of some of the industry's greatests.

They say that if you want to learn, "you should never be the smartest person in the room". And by working through this blueprint, you've given yourself a head start – because you've learned from professionals who've spent years fine-tuning their knowledge of their respective fields.

There's no better foundation for your direct bookings business; I'm sure you can agree with me on that.

To continue this epic flow that you're in, be sure to watch all the tutorial videos and interviews that are part of the online course, which accompanies this Blueprint. These have been created especially for you (from scratch), and they'll only add more value to your direct bookings toolkit.

I'd also love for you to join The Boostly Book Club on Facebook, where you might cross digital paths with some of our very own authors (it's as good as meeting celebs, really). You'll get the chance to ask them questions in real-time, while we continue to discuss and enjoy other business books within the group.

Lastly, it would mean the world to me and my team of authors if you left a review of this **Blueprint** on Amazon, so we can help more hosts and hospitality business owners realise that there are other (better) ways to grow a short-term rental business than relying on OTAs. Leaving a review will take all of two minutes, but the positive impact on our industry could be enormous.

I invite each and every one of you to get in touch via DM on Instagram or shoot an email to **info@boostly.co.uk** with literally any feedback or thoughts about this book. As always, it's been a labour of love – but it's your honest opinions that help me improve each day.

So, you're officially part of #TeamBoostly now – and it feels pretty fantastic to have you under our roof with us! Remember, for more direct bookings goodness, you can order my debut book **The Book Direct Playbook** on Amazon too (or even if you just miss the sound of my writing, ha). Scan the QR code below to find out more.

Huge well done for getting this far – here's to more direct bookings, and the power of building together.

COMING SOON

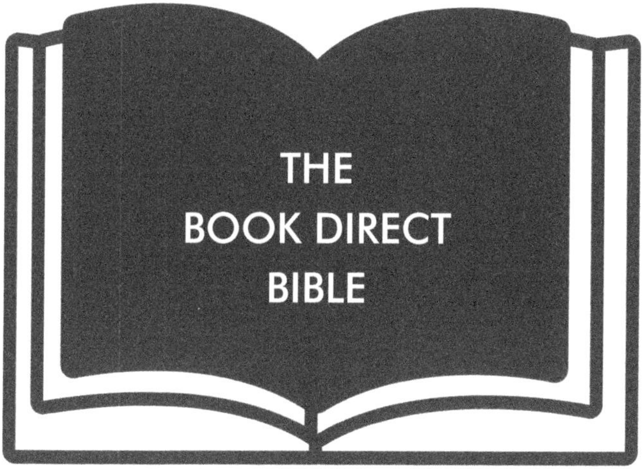

SOURCES

Dtravel:

1 https://www.cross-croscombe.co.uk/blog/bed-breakfast-global-phenomenon/#:~:text=Bed%20and%20breakfasts%20have%20been,breakfast%20to%20those%20overnight%20guests.

2 https://www.cnbc.com/2020/04/22/airbnb-hosts-getting-almost-nothing-from-250-million-relief-fund.html

3 https://airhostsforum.com/t/info-on-airbnb-shares-for-hosts-usa-only/44644/11

4 https://seetransparent.com/blog/vacation-rental-direct-bookings

5 https://www.rsisinternational.org/IJRSI/Issue31/75-78.pdf

6 https://web.archive.org/web/19980113070534/http://vrbo.com:80/vrbo/

7 https://web.archive.org/web/19980113070534/http://vrbo.com:80/vrbo/

8 http://ijcsit.com/docs/Volume%205/vol5issue06/ijcsit20140506265.pdf

9 As of July 2022. https://datareportal.com/global-digital-overview#:~:text=A%20total%20of%205.03%20billion,12%20months%20to%20July%202022.

10 In the paper, he describes an internet where web pages are structured in such a way that computers and software can understand content in the same way that people can (i.e. semantically) and be able to carry out sophisticated tasks for people just by users expressing intent. However, because indexing and creating taxonomies and meaning for computers and software to understand is an incredibly complex and challenging problem to solve, this version of Web 3.0 has remained largely unrealised.
https://www-sop.inria.fr/acacia/cours/essi2006/Scientific%20American_%20Feature%20Article_%20The%20Semantic%20Web_%20May%202001.pdf

11 https://www.weforum.org/agenda/2021/11/millennials-world-regional-breakdown/#:~:text=Author%2C%20Visual%20Capitalist-,Millennials%20are%20now%20the%20largest%20adult%20cohort%20worldwide.,educated%20and%20are%20increasingly%20influential.

12 https://truelist.co/blog/generation-z-statistics/

13 https://explodingtopics.com/blog/blockchain-stats

14 https://www.pymnts.com/travel-payments/2022/the-digital-merchant-2022-cryptocurrency-payments-take-travel-new-directions/#:~:text=Otero%20called%20it%20%E2%80%9Cthe%20first,bookings%20are%20paid%20with%20crypto.

15 https://blog.travala.com/category/reports/

Touch Stay:

"10 Vacation Rental Statistics That May Surprise You." *Bookfull*, 20 May 2019, https://bookfull.com/2018/02/01/vacation-rental-statistics/.

Dack:

McKain, Scott. Create Distinction: *What to Do When "'Great'" Isn't Good Enough to Grow Your Business.* Greenleaf Book Group Press, 2013.

Pine II, Joseph, and James Gilmore. *The Experience Economy, With a New Preface by the Authors: Competing for Customer Time, Attention, and Money.* Revised, Harvard Business Review Press, 2019.

ThinkwithGoogle. "How Mobile Influences Travel Decision Making in Can't-Wait-to-Explore Moments." *Think with Google*, 3 Sept. 2020, www.thinkwithgoogle.com/consumer-insights/consumer-journey/mobile-influence-travel-decision-making-explore-moments.

"Conifer's 5E Framework." *Conifer Research*, 20 Jan. 2022, coniferresearch.com/5e-framework.

"5 Ways to Stay Ahead of the Competition – Podium." *https://www.podium.com*, Podium, www.podium.com/ebooks/5-ways-to-stay-ahead-of-the-competition. Accessed 7 Aug. 2022.

Meyer, Danny. *Setting the Table: The Transforming Power of Hospitality in Business.* Reprint, Kindle ed., Harper Collins, 2008

https://www.brandwatch.com/reports/2020-best-brands-for-cx/view/

Berger, Jonah. *Contagious: Why Things Catch On.* Reprint, Simon and Schuster, 2016.

https://www.medallia.com/resource/the-customer-experience-tipping-point-an-ipsos-and-medallia-study/